**Advance Praise**

What you have between your hands is a [illegible] addition to resources available to teachers and students of theology. It is a brilliant way of teaching the church about itself; one more outstanding achievement by accomplished pastor and theologian Rev. Matt Snowden and important contribution of Rev. Joshua Hays! I especially find useful and informative listing ingredients of the dough and giving ample explanation about each from the Bible and from other cultural landmarks. Church leaders have plentiful to learn as they read and browse through its pages; students will to learn more as they read about elements that make the dough—i.e., beliefs, attitudes, values, goals, and practices. The outcome is surely reviving one's personal journey to seek the Kingdom of God by knowing Christ or by starting the path. It is especially useful for people and the church in the Middle East, and we sure benefit a great deal from translating to Arabic, a forthcoming project of our publishing ministry, Lord willing!

*—Dr. Nabil Costa*
*CEO, Lebanese Society for Educational and Social Development (LSESD)*
*and founder of SKILD Center*

As a college basketball coach, I work every day to instill a culture of joy among my players and staff. This book helps Christian leaders think strategically about the five ingredients vital to every culture.

*—Scott Drew*
*Head Coach, Men's Basketball*
*Baylor University*

In a world where superficiality seems to be the order of the day, Joshua Hays and Matt Snowden lead us to a deep well of spiritual refreshing and bid us to drink deeply. Through experience and reflection, they offer profound and practical insights that will challenge and inspire leaders to develop the kind of spaces that foster Christian community under the Word of God, through the Spirit of Christ. This book should be in the hands of every leader immediately.

*—Tyshawn Gardner, PhD*
*Associate Professor of Christian and Biblical Studies*
*Samford University*

Consider this book a timely multivitamin for congregational vitality. Do you need a boost? Matt Snowden and Josh Hayes give us real help for being the church now. Valuing individuality they explore Beliefs, Attitudes, Values, Goals and the resulting Practices in congregations. It is a toolbox for building soul culture to nurture and energize ministry. Through humor, thoughtful reflection, scriptural grounding and practical steps, Hayes and Snowden show the inspiration and perspiration they have shared in the challenge of ministry today.

*—Suzii Paynter March*
*Former Executive Coordinator, Cooperative Baptist Fellowship*

Matt Snowden and Joshua Hays have written a terrific book. It is a treasure for anyone who would seriously invest in building the "soul culture" of a congregation. This book unpacks the realities of ministry and helps give a framework for addressing them. I began reading out of genuine interest. I continued reading because it fed my soul.

*—Jim Martin*
*Vice President, Harding School of Theology*

Inside *Soul Culture* you're about to find a passionate project that will call you wrestle with a living God and the churches life in relation to this living God. Joshua Hays and Matt Snowden are wonderful guides. They give so many handles and examples to make their ideas and larger points come to life. This is a very helpful book.

*—Andrew Root*
*Author of the* Ministry in a Secular Age *series*

The church is a Spirit-created institution. Though an outworking of God's heavenly presence, it is manifestly a community of people who live and move in this world, with all its human problems and differences. It takes the Spirit and our willingness to follow God to be one. This book will help us discern where the Spirit is leading so that we may better fulfill God's purpose for us as a community and find oneness through our God-given diversity.

*—Dr. Ralph D. West*
*Founder and Senior Pastor of The Church Without Walls*
*Brookhollow Baptist Church*
*Houston, Texas*

# SOUL CULTURE

Smyth & Helwys Publishing, Inc.
6316 Peake Road
Macon, Georgia 31210-3960
1-800-747-3016


*Library of Congress Cataloging-in-Publication Data on file*

# SOUL CULTURE

## *Stewarding the Five Ingredients of Our Common Life*

Matt Snowden and Joshua Hays

*To the people of First Baptist Church, Waco, Texas*

# Acknowledgments

Many friends and partners have contributed to this project, and we humbly acknowledge our gratitude. Thank you to the congregation of First Baptist Church Waco, the first to listen and offer feedback to refine these ideas. Special thanks are due to church members Joel Allison and Dr. John Anderson for their generous insights regarding organizational leadership. We are likewise grateful to Professor David Bebbington for urging us to consider the kingship of every believer alongside our shared priesthood and prophethood with Christ; we're delighted to pastor your Texas church. Matt offers his thanks to participants in the 2021 Paisano Baptist Encampment, where he taught much of this material. Your feedback has also enriched our communication.

Our staff team at FBC Waco is a blessing. It's a joy to serve alongside each one of you. Thanks especially to Ryan Russell, associate pastor for college and missions, for hosting dialogue about the ingredients of soul culture on *The Lightbulb Factory* podcast and to Autumn Seacat, ministry associate, for reading early drafts of the manuscript and offering constructive feedback and discussion prompts. We extend special thanks to ministry colleagues Steve Bezner, Maddie Rarick, and Ralph Douglas West for sharing their insights in the final chapter. We're blessed to count you as our friends and co-laborers.

This project has taken on its present form through the professional assistance and encouragement of the Smyth & Helwys Publishing team. We thank them, particularly publisher Keith Gammons. We're also grateful for the illustrations provided by Heath Holland. A grant from the Lilly Foundation's "Called to Lives of Meaning and Purpose" initiative allowed us to give this project our time and attention. Thanks to the Lilly team and particularly the staff of Baylor University's Institute for Faith and Learning for administering the Soundings Project, our church's grant hub. Thanks also to the other Soundings Project churches and their leaders that have enriched our discussions around vocation and congregational life.

Finally, thank you to our families for supporting us throughout this work. Your encouragement, support, and love sustain us always, especially through seasons of additional endeavor. We are both better men and better pastors because of you. We offer this book in gratitude for the sacrifices that you have made to bring it to completion and in prayerful hope that it will strengthen and encourage the church of our Lord Jesus in all its manifold local expressions.

*Gratefully,*
*Matt Snowden and Joshua Hays*
*Waco, Texas*
*July 2023*

# Contents

# Preface

Cultures belong to communities, and no community is more precious than Christ's church. The New Testament qualifies the word "church" in two ways: the church *of* the Lord Jesus Christ, and the church *in* a particular place. The apostles wrote to specific congregations in Corinth, Colossae, and Crete to remind them that they all collectively comprise the church of the risen Jesus.

These twin realities continue to define the church today. The one church of Christ throughout time and space takes concrete expression as the church in D.C, the church in Danville, and the church in Detroit. We write from the church at the corner of 5th and Webster in Waco, Texas. Each of these communities manifests its own unique culture, and together these cultures contribute to the church in its fullest expression.

Our prayerful hope is for this book to encourage and equip richer ministry *within* your local community. We believe that the best way to accomplish that task is to consider the ideas discussed within community. While some of you might read the entire book aloud while sitting in a circle of friends, we invite you to read each chapter on your own, spend some time digesting it, and then come together for some community conversation around the big ideas. We've provided some tools to help.

At the end of each chapter, you'll find two supplemental resources. The first is a worksheet with questions for reflection. Using these worksheets individually will guide you further into each chapter's big ideas. Worksheets are printed within the book but also available as a PDF to download and print from **helwys.com/media/Soul_Culture_Worksheets.pdf**. The second resource is a group discussion guide. Here's where the community gets together. We hope that you'll use these prompts to shape conversation around *Soul Culture* themes. The guides recommend questions and activities for groups of all sizes. We designed these tools to probe some of the unique gifts and opportunities of *your* congregation so that you may better serve the call of the gospel. You may want to use them as a nine-session curriculum or structure a weekend leadership retreat around this material. If you'd like for us to come sip coffee and talk about soul culture with your congregation, just let us know!

We humbly offer these resources to you in the hope that they further equip you and your communities for the work of ministry. We're grateful to share a holy calling with you because we share a gracious Lord.

*—Matt and Josh*

# 1. Working a Batch of Dough

> *Clean out the old yeast so you can be a new batch of dough, given that you're supposed to be unleavened bread. Christ our Passover lamb has been sacrificed....*
>
> 1 Corinthians 5:7[1]

> *Since there is one loaf of bread, we who are many are one body, because we all share the one loaf of bread.*
>
> 1 Corinthians 10:17

A perfect pizza dough is a work of art. Gus Lisi is an artist. As a little boy in Strangolagalli, Italy, Gus watched airplanes leave white contrails in the blue sky and prayed to God that one day an airplane would take him to America. His prayers were answered. Gus immigrated as a child and grew into a man in the United States. He served in the Navy, and the Navy eventually brought him to Meridian, Mississippi.

Always the dreamer, Gus planned his life after military service while he was enlisted. He loved food and hospitality and the joy that a gathering table could kindle. When he left the Navy, Gus began a career in the restaurant business. Eventually he opened a series of profitable Subway sandwich shops. This success allowed him to launch his passion project in 1999, Nick and Al's New York Style Pizzeria.

Nick and Al's paid homage to Gus's grandfather Luigi, so pride filled the pizzeria. Nick and Al's would not serve fast food or bad food in Luigi's name. A restaurant that takes time to get the food right but also caters to young families is a restaurant with a problem to overcome. How do you keep impatient kids from starting a small-scale riot while waiting on food as they smell the glories of Strangolagalli, Italy? Gus, ever the empathic

---

1. Unless otherwise noted, all Scripture quotations are taken from the Common English Bible (CEB) 2011.

businessman, figured it out. You get the kids in on it. You invite them into the whole experience.

Nick and Al's has an open-concept kitchen. Kids are mesmerized watching bakers toss pizza dough high into the air. Gus subtly teaches these captivated kids that food should be handmade and crafted with love. When restaurant hosts seat families at their tables, they immediately give the kids a lump of dough to mimic the action in the kitchen. They work the lump, roll it out, and toss it high into the air. Laughter and learning always fill the pizzeria, not to mention the best New York-style pizza in the state of Mississippi.

Nick and Al's New York Style Pizzeria offers the church quite a few important lessons about fellowship and discipleship. Many of these illustrations are easy to spot. The core lesson, however, may take a bit more work.

The lump of dough is the centerpiece of the pizzeria. The lump of dough is also a central biblical metaphor for the church. In 1 Corinthians Paul uses the lump of dough to teach the Corinthian church about their common identity as a Christian community. They are one. They are also many. They are one bread and one body made of multiple ingredients, processes, time, and heat. They are whole and are also becoming. When bakers work a batch of dough, they are holding in their hands a symbol of the Christian faith, whether or not they recognize it.

Paul was not the last church leader to use the image of the lump of dough to teach the church about itself. A turn-of-the-century Baptist leader named J. B. Gambrell wrote a memorable essay titled "Working a Batch of Dough." Gambrell labored to instill a sense of cooperative ministry among early Southern Baptists. In today's terms, he worked with both Cracker Barrel and Whole Foods congregations. He wanted them to mature together and to collaborate in God's work. He wrote with hope,

> If we are wise, we will work our dough. There is no greater nor more hopeful task before us than so to culture our people as to bring them to a New Testament way of thinking and feeling. This culture is perhaps as much needed in the so-called highest circles as in the lowest. I am not thinking now of worldly culture, but soul culture, growing out of a deep experimental knowledge of God.[2]

2. J. B. Gambrell, "Working a Batch of Dough," in *Parable and Precept* (New York: Revell, 1917), 63.

We can wisely work our dough by "soul culturing" our people. *Soul culture* is a helpful concept that describes a New Testament way of thinking, feeling, wanting, planning, and doing. A church is a lump of dough. A church is a soul culture. Shaping this culture is a great and hopeful task for church leaders because culture is crucial.

Legendary management consultant Peter Drucker allegedly said, "Culture eats strategy for breakfast." The line has been used so many times it has taken on a life of its own. Culture, whatever it is, is widely accepted as the key to an organization's effectiveness.

Church leaders have long known that culture is crucial. We have just had a tough time getting our hands on it. If we can't get our hands on it, we can't work it. Peter Scazzero wrote in *The Emotionally Healthy Leader*, "Culture is that imprecise something, the invisible presence or personality of a place that can be difficult to describe without actually experiencing it. It is often more readily felt than articulated."[3]

Soul culture is indeed felt. Perhaps that feeling is why Walter Wink wrote of the "angel" of a church. When we feel a church's soul culture, we meet its "angel." Wink wrote,

> The angel seemed to be the corporate personality of the church, its ethos or spirit or essence. Looking back over my experience of churches, I realized that each did indeed have a unique personality. Furthermore, that personality was real. It wasn't what we call a "personification" like Uncle Sam or the Quaker on the box of oats. But it didn't seem like a distinct spiritual entity with an independent existence either. The angel of a church was apparently the spirituality of a particular church. You can sense the "angel" when you worship at a church. But you also encounter the angel in the church's committee meetings and even in its architecture.[4]

David Bolin and Terry York spoke in similar ways when they wrote of the "voice" of the congregation. When we feel a church's soul culture, we hear the voice of the congregation. Their work is helpful because they show the union of God's grace and the collective human experience that forms a particular congregation. In describing their project, they said,

---

3. Peter Scazzero, *The Emotionally Healthy Leader* (Grand Rapids, MI: Zondervan, 2013), 213.

4. Walter Wink, *The Powers That Be: Theology for a New Millennium* (New York: Doubleday, 1998), 3–4.

> What is the voice of your congregation? The congregation sings an important song, yet its voice is more than an echo of the Master. The congregation's voice is the voice of testimony, praise, and prayer, rising from the lives and hearts of its individual members as a great congregational chorus that harmonizes by the grace and in the Spirit of God.[5]

The voice of the congregation is a mixture of God's voice and our voices, grace and the human response to grace.

Angels. Voices. Have we lost our minds? This notion seems mystical, and to a degree it is. Comprehending soul culture requires spiritual sensitivity and discernment. It does not, however, have to be imprecise or antirational. We hope to show you that a congregation's "soul culture" can be articulated as well as felt, dissected as well as discerned.

Working a batch of congregational dough begins with the basic ingredients. A simple online search or an old school flip through a dictionary suggests that cultures large and small are made of basic elements. Five key constituent parts seem to form cultures. These ingredients are beliefs, values, attitudes, goals, and practices.

Try this exercise at home: Get out your Bible. Read all the New Testament epistles. Ask yourself what is being addressed paragraph by paragraph, pericope by pericope. It is likely that you will see the writer dealing with beliefs, values, attitudes, goals, and/or practices. The New Testament authors applied the good news of Jesus Christ to all these elements because the churches that they addressed were soul cultures. The apostles were "culturing" the congregations. They were laboring to bring these early churches to a gospel way of thinking, wanting, feeling, planning, and acting.

When we conducted our own at-home experiment with the five elements of culture and the epistles, a light went on for us. We learned how we can be intentional about understanding and shaping our church's culture. To serve the whole, we have to recognize and understand its parts.

To test our thoughts further, we visited our friend Larry Lyon. Dr. Lyon is vice provost and dean of the graduate school at Baylor University and a respected sociologist of religion. We laid out our notes and made our case. We asked Dr. Lyon if we fairly represented the constituent elements of culture. He laid his napkin on the table, leaned forward, and gave us his scholarly opinion: "Yep. That's pretty much it." Culture is crucial. Culture

5. Terry W. York and C. David Bolin, *The Voice of Our Congregation: Seeking and Celebrating God's Song for Us* (Macon, GA: Celebrating Grace, 2017), back cover.

doesn't have to be imprecise or go unarticulated. We can understand the ingredients. We can work the dough.

We believe that an intuitive and intentional approach to working the dough of soul culture is to be commended and pursued. Dream for a moment that you are an NFL quarterback. As you play the game, the action runs at lightning speed. You work based on sight, sound, muscle memory, blood, sweat, and tears. Your training and intuition combine on the field to lead your team. Let's call this the Sunday approach. Monday follows Sunday every single week. For an NFL quarterback, film follows field. Let's call this the Monday morning approach. Football players and coaches watch tons of game film. The most important camera angle is called the All-22, aka the Coaches' Angle. A camera mounted high above the field captures this footage. It allows the viewer to see all twenty-two players on the field in a single shot. This bird's-eye view gives a sense of the game that is never experienced during the heat of a play. Players and coaches commit themselves to cool analysis of All-22 video so that they will be prepared for the speed and limited vision on the field.

Church leaders lead from the front. Our calling is to play side by side with others. We read and apply Scripture, and in doing so we help culture the congregation as they do the same. We are Sunday morning leaders. Church leaders also have a special role as overseers. We are Monday morning leaders. We need an All-22 view. We also need to help our churches achieve this vision. Taking a cool look at the elements of our congregation's soul culture will allow us to articulate that culture so that we can shape it for God's glory and our good.

## Case Study: The Idol Food Challenge in 1 Corinthians 8-10

If you are not quite ready to run the five elements of soul culture through all the epistles, 1 Corinthians 8–10 serves as a helpful test case. The Corinthian church was vexed over the consumption of food offered to idols. Could they eat it? Should they abstain? Some members of the church had been eating this food all their lives. To abstain would mark a substantive change of life. Paul could have simply rendered a verdict for them. He could have become the Nancy Reagan of the ancient world and said, "Just say no!" He chose instead to culture the congregation by addressing not simply a practice but the beliefs, attitudes, values, and goals that connected to it. He worked with the Corinthian congregation holistically and comprehensively. He led them to a place of decision regarding something that had profound consequences for their daily life and witness.

## *Beliefs*

N. T. Wright once said, "Theology is the backbone of a healthy church."[6] We embrace faithful theology when Christ is our starting point. Christ is central to Paul's teaching about idol food. He says in 1 Corinthians 10:15-17,

> I'm talking to you like you are sensible people. Think about what I'm saying. Isn't the cup of blessing that we bless a sharing in the blood of Christ? Isn't the loaf of bread that we break a sharing in the body of Christ? Since there is one loaf of bread, we who are many are one body, because we all share the one loaf of bread.

Paul is addressing the Corinthian church's beliefs.

Paul wanted the church to understand that their union, their common life as a church, was rooted in more than a voluntary association. They were not members of a club. They had a special union, a oneness, because of the blood of Jesus. They were one body because of the broken body of Jesus. They were one loaf. In 1 Corinthians 5:7 Paul describes the church as one unleavened lump of dough because Christ the Passover lamb has been sacrificed. Their oneness comes from partaking of the one bread, Jesus.

Paul linked beliefs about atonement and unity with the practice of abstaining from idol meat. Eating should not divide the church because the church is one in Christ. They should abstain from drinking the cup of demons because they are blessed to drink from the cup of the Lord. God, in mercy and grace, gave life to each member of the Corinthian congregation. In love, God gathered them in community.

We can do theology because God turned to us in love and made Godself known in Christ, the holy Scriptures, and the proclamation of the church. The most awe-inspiring aspect of God's revelation is the cross. The crucifixion is the meeting place of God and a weary humanity. For Paul and the other New Testament writers, everything goes back to the truth that Jesus died for sinners according to the Scriptures. This central locating theme is the cornerstone that holds the church together. So, when addressing a real challenge in the congregation, Paul turned to theology.

---

6. N. T. Wright, *Paul: A Biography* (New York: HarperOne, 2020), 428–29.

When he could have sent a memo with a freshly written rule, he opted to teach. He reminded the Corinthians, and us, who Christ is and what he has done. He reminded them that their lives were due him, and because of this debt they had clear obligations to one another. Paul kneaded the dough of Corinth's soul culture by working first with its primary ingredient—beliefs.

## Attitudes

Attitude is the second ingredient worked into the dough in 1 Corinthians. The high and hopeful task of culturing a congregation is a matter of thinking *and* feeling. Paul brilliantly ties these together in 1 Corinthians 8:8-13:

> Food won't bring us close to God. We're not missing out if we don't eat, and we don't have any advantage if we do eat. But watch out or else this freedom of yours might be a problem for those who are weak. Suppose someone sees you (the person who has knowledge) eating in an idol's temple. Won't the person with a weak conscience be encouraged to eat the meat sacrificed to false gods? The weak brother or sister for whom Christ died is destroyed by your knowledge. You sin against Christ if you sin against your brothers and sisters and hurt their weak consciences this way. This is why, if food causes the downfall of my brother or sister, I won't eat meat ever again, or else I may cause my brother or sister to fall.

Paul clearly addressed the attitudes of the Corinthian believers. Some members of this congregation believed that if they had enough "knowledge," then they were free to live as they liked without having to deal with their decision's impact on their family in Christ. Paul wanted the members of the church to feel like each of them was a sibling "for whom Christ died." Gordon Fee described the situation this way:

> Their problem is primarily attitudinal. They think Christian conduct is predicated on *gnōsis* (knowledge) and that knowledge gives the *exousia* (rights/freedom) to act as they will in this matter. Paul has another view: The content of their knowledge is only partially correct; but more importantly, *gnōsis* is not the ground of Christian behavior, love is.[7]

The Holy Spirit works to shape our attitudes according to the gospel. When we worship God, study Scripture, pray together, and serve alongside

---

7. Gordon D. Fee, *The First Epistle to the Corinthians*, New International Commentary on the New Testament (Grand Rapids, MI: Eerdmans, 1987), 363.

one another, God transforms our attitudes into ever-closer conformity with the Spirit of Christ within us.

## *Values*

Corporate jargon has co-opted the word "values" to the point that it often makes hearers' eyes glaze over. Managerial consultants and marketing gurus often describe qualities like excellence and efficiency as values. Churches frequently adopt a shallow definition of values drawn from the corporate word salad. Paul addressed values, the third ingredient of soul culture, in a different way. He appealed to shared values in the midst of the idol food conversation by reminding the church that he was engaging them because he had been entrusted with stewardship. The idea of stewardship may be the key to living gospel-driven values. Listen to what Paul says in 1 Corinthians 9:14-17:

> In the same way, the Lord commanded that those who preach the gospel should get their living from the gospel. But I haven't taken advantage of this. And I'm not writing this so that it will be done for me. It's better for me to die than to lose my right to brag about this! If I preach the gospel, I have no reason to brag, since I'm obligated to do it. I'm in trouble if I don't preach the gospel. If I do this voluntarily, I get rewarded for it. But if I'm forced to do it, then I've been charged with a responsibility.

Paul believed that it was completely appropriate to support ministers financially. Yet in his relationship with the church in Corinth, he opted out of this financial arrangement. That congregation's view of money and upward mobility made financial support an unhelpful entanglement, a stumbling block to his ministry of proclamation and discipleship. He chose instead to work with his hands to support himself and minister to them free of charge. He wanted to underscore that God was their patron as well as his. God was their source and provider. They could not hustle God and use their position or possessions to control the congregation. Paul's personal note about work, pay, and stewardship was not a random thought scribbled down out of place; it was an important part of the idol food conversation. As Paul shaped the soul culture of the church, he had to deal with values. As the Corinthian Christians approached the Lord's table and grappled with ethical decisions, they had to do so as God's stewards.

One of life's biggest questions is "Whose am I?" This question likely even supersedes "Who am I?" The most frequent reflexive answer is, "I belong to me." In his wise and helpful book *You Are Not Your Own*, Alan Noble unmasks this answer to reveal a withering lie:

> This is the fundamental lie of modernity: that we are our own. Until we see this lie for what it is, until we work to uproot it from our culture and replant a conception of human persons as belonging to God and not ourselves, most of our efforts at improving the world will be glorified Band-Aids.
>
> The first question and answer in the Heidelberg Catechism reads:
>
> Q. What is your only comfort in life and death?
> A. That I am not my own,
> but belong with body and soul,
> both in life and in death,
> to my faithful savior, Jesus Christ.
>
> A proper understanding of our personhood requires we recognize that we are not our own. At our core we belong to Christ.[8]

We are not our own. Paul said so directly to the Corinthian church: "Or don't you know that your body is a temple of the Holy Spirit who is in you? Don't you know that you have the Holy Spirit from God, and you don't belong to yourselves? You have been bought and paid for, so honor God with your body" (1 Cor 6:19-20). Belonging to Christ is the foundation of stewardship and the animating principle behind gospel-driven values.

## *Goals*

As Paul worked the dough in Corinth, he was careful to mix in goals, the fourth key ingredient of soul culture. The Corinthian church was not a directionless community. As their spiritual father (1 Cor 4:15), Paul could not allow them to live aimlessly. Instead, he reminded the church at Corinth that they were constituted by God's grace to seek the kingdom of Christ by knowing Christ and making him known. Paul himself embodied this gospel ambition. He used his personal example to shape congregational culture in Corinth.

---

8. Alan Noble, *You Are Not Your Own: Belonging to God in an Inhuman World* (Downers Grove, IL: IVP, 2021), 5.

Paul wrote in 1 Corinthians 9:19, "Although I'm free from all people, I make myself a slave to all people, to recruit more of them." Paul had a burning ambition, and his ambition was the gospel. He wanted the story of God's transforming grace to extend to more and more people, resulting in thanksgiving and glory to God. This goal of his life was rooted in the goal Jesus gave to all the church in the Great Commission (Matt 28:19-20) and Great Commandment (Matt 22:36-40). Paul was purposeful about his living. He gave a fantastic illustration of this drive in 1 Corinthians 9:26: "So now this is how I run—not without a clear goal in sight. I fight like a boxer in the ring, not like someone who is shadowboxing." Paul did not want his hearers in Corinth to waste their lives. He did not want them to squander their days in fistfights with the air. As he cultured the church, he refocused their aim. He rehearsed their goal. He brought them back to the stark gift of the gospel. Spirit-inspired ambition breathes life into the soul culture of a healthy church.

## *Practices*

In his bestselling biography of Leonardo Da Vinci, Walter Isaacson says, "Vision without execution is hallucination."[9] Leonardo was a dreamer, but he also knew how to concretize his ideas through inventions. Paul was cut from the same cloth. He was profoundly against a hallucinating church. Beliefs, values, attitudes, and goals ought to result in practices, both in first-century Corinth and today. These practices comprise the final ingredient in our batch of dough. In 1 Corinthians 8–10, the apostle commends an exemplary set of concrete practices that served as artifacts and services of the congregation's soul culture.

We see the practice of evangelism. Paul said in 1 Corinthians 9:23, "All the things I do are for the sake of the gospel, so I can be a partner with it." Paul had a vision to make Christ known, and he concretized this goal through the practice of publishing the good news.

In 1 Corinthians 10:1-15 we see the practice of Scripture study. Paul took the church at Corinth on a journey through the Old Testament. He showed them that Christ was the nourishing rock in the wilderness. Any doctrine of Scripture needs to take in the stunning ideas of Romans 15:4: "Whatever was written in the past was written for our instruction so that we could have hope through endurance and through the encouragement of the scriptures." Paul was encouraging the congregation through the Scriptures.

9. Walter Isaacson, *Leonardo da Vinci* (New York: Simon and Schuster, 2017), 5.

The church in Corinth also practiced the Lord's Table. We read in 1 Corinthians 10:16, "Isn't the cup of blessing that we bless a sharing in the blood of Christ? Isn't the loaf of bread that we break a sharing in the body of Christ?" The church gathered at the table, and the practice of eating the Lord's Supper together spoke to the theological and ethical questions that were impacting the church's soul culture. Here we return to the presenting issue, the question of whether to consume meat offered up to idols.

The church was called to practice abstinence from idol meat under most circumstances. Ultimately, eating this meat was out of bounds for the Corinthians because of love for one another. Abstinence may seem like a totally passive practice, but it is not. Abstaining demands considerable positive energy. In order to accomplish such a practice, one needs to be established by sound beliefs, possessed by a Christlike attitude, governed by gospel values, and driven by a great purpose. Paul could have simply responded to the question of idol meat by saying, ". . . my dear friends, run away from the worship of false gods!" (1 Cor 10:14). Instead of this memo method, he wisely worked the batch of dough. He brought all the ingredients of soul culture together and allowed strength to give strength to strength.

In 1 Corinthians 8–10 we have the example of a church leader working a batch of dough. Paul had a Sunday approach. He lived up close to the congregation in Corinth within the messiness of the day by day. He loved them and struggled with them and practiced the gospel with them. Paul also had a cool-headed Monday approach. The epistle as a ministry tool was a technology that allowed for the All-22 coach's vision. Paul's letters are artifacts of fieldwork theology. Like gonzo journalist Hunter Thompson, Paul made no claim to objectivity; instead, he wrote from a vantage point immersed within the circumstances he addressed. He was a pastor. He defined reality for the congregation that he loved and addressed every ingredient of their congregational culture. He serves as a model for all church leaders who want to engage the high and hopeful task of culturing a church to reflect the kingdom of Christ.

We likewise write as participant-observers. We reflect as pastors eager to bring the reflections of our Monday perspective to bear on our Sunday experiences. In the chapters that follow, we will develop each ingredient of soul culture more thoroughly. We take our guidance from the Scriptures each step of the way. God's revelation defines and transforms our beliefs, attitudes, values, goals, and practices as both individuals and congregations.

We intend to encourage you with the Scriptures so that you will endure and flourish in service to the congregation which God has called you to serve.

Chapter 1

# Working a Batch of Dough

**Questions for Further Reflection**

1. J. B. Gambrell claimed that a church's "soul culture" grows from "a deep, experimental knowledge of God."[1] What does this "experimental knowledge" (we might say "experiential" today) mean? How have you personally experienced God? How have these encounters shaped your life?

_____

_____

_____

_____

_____

2. Take a few minutes to read through 1 Corinthians 8–10. Jot down each challenge that Paul addresses and each recommendation in the chart below:

| Challenges | Recommendations |
|---|---|
|  |  |

3. Now return to the chart and consider whether each entry is a matter of beliefs, attitudes, values, goals, or practices. You might want to mark each one with a symbol like these:

| Beliefs | ✝ |
|---|---|
| Attitudes | ☺ |
| Values | $ |
| Goals | ◎ |
| Practices | 🖐 |

If these symbols are helpful, you may want to use them for shorthand notes as you continue to read.

4. Which of the five "ingredients" of culture (beliefs, attitudes, values, goals, and practices) are the most intuitive to you? If you're unsure, think about which one(s) you talk about the most. When faced with a problem, which one(s) do you tend to pursue first to find a solution?

_____

_____

_____

_____

5. Which ingredient(s) are less familiar to you? Why do you think you've given less attention to these elements?

_____

_____

_____

_____

1. J. B. Gambrell, "Working a Batch of Dough," in _Parable and Precept_ (New York: Revell, 1917), 63.

# Chapter 1: Working a Batch of Dough

## *Group Discussion Guide*

Start with a meal at Nick and Al's in Meridian, Mississippi.

If you can't make it to Nick and Al's, begin by watching a quick video about breadmaking. There are plenty of possibilities online. We suggest the first few minutes of "The Magic of Bread Making" by Tasty on YouTube.[10]

Bread is an evocative image. What memories and associations does it call to your mind?

- Family recipes or memories like Nick and Al's Pizzeria?
- Your own baking experiences (or at least watching baking shows on TV)?
- How about bread in the Bible?

Give participants time to respond and then offer a few of the examples and texts below if they haven't been mentioned yet.

- *Unleavened bread at Passover (Exodus 12:8, 14-20)*
- *Manna in the wilderness (Exodus 16)*
- *Flatbread offered to the Lord in the tabernacle and temple (Leviticus 24:5-9)*
- *Jesus's prayer for "our daily bread," emblematic of all our daily needs (Matthew 6:11)*
- *Bread and wine at the Lord's Table (1 Corinthians 11:23-26)*

Jesus reinterpreted the unleavened bread of Passover at his last supper with the disciples. The church commemorates this meal at the Lord's Table, proclaiming his death until he comes again and gathers his people for the marriage feast of the Lamb (Rev 19:9). This image of bread bookends the entire biblical story of redemption across both testaments. It also recalls personal memories of tables shared with family or friends.

*Discuss the following questions with the group.*

1. In 1 Corinthians 5:7, Paul describes the church as one unleavened lump of dough because Christ the Passover Lamb has been sacrificed. What does it mean for the church to live in continual celebration of Passover?

---

10. Tasty, "The Magic of Bread Making," YouTube, available at youtube.com/watch?v=EGbNI26PPYg.

2. Bread is one thing, and it is many things. Do you tend to think of your church more as a unity or as a collection of parts? Is your congregation a loaf or a collection of ingredients? How could the opposite perspective enhance your understanding?

3. Along with flour, water, salt, and yeast, one of the most important ingredients in baking is *time*. Fresh dough needs time to rise before the baker can form it into a loaf. Too much or too little time can ruin the batch, so a wise baker is attentive to the process. Baking requires even more time and attention. Since time is so crucial, a momentary snapshot can never tell the story of a good loaf. What role does time play in developing the culture of a church?

4. J. B. Gambrell claimed that a church's "soul culture" grows from "a deep, experimental knowledge of God."[11] What does this "experimental knowledge" (we might say "experiential" today) mean to you? How has your church experienced God at work in your midst? How have you experienced God personally? *(Record answers on a whiteboard or flip chart. If you're using a whiteboard, snap a photo before erasing it. You'll want to record these stories of God at work and return to them later.)*

5. Peter Drucker claims, "Culture eats strategy for breakfast." If he's right, do we abandon strategy entirely? How should culture and strategy relate?

6. Divide into five groups and read the letters to the seven churches in Revelation 2–3. Assign each group an element of "soul culture" (beliefs, attitudes, values, goals, and practices), and invite them to identify each church's reflection of that element based on the text. *(Allow about ten minutes for discussion within groups, and then come together and share what each group has noticed.)*

7. Read 1 Corinthians 10:15-17 aloud:

> I'm talking to you like you are sensible people. Think about what I'm saying. Isn't the cup of blessing that we bless a sharing in the blood of Christ? Isn't the loaf of bread that we break a sharing in the body of

---

11. J. B. Gambrell, "Working a Batch of Dough," in *Parable and Precept* (New York: Revell, 1917), 63.

> Christ? Since there is one loaf of bread, we who are many are one body, because we all share the one loaf of bread.

Paul appealed to the Corinthian church on the basis of their shared beliefs. Why do you think he chose to engage them that way? Why not send a memo or remind them of a rule to correct their deficient behavior?

8. Scripture teaches beliefs embedded within stories. When the prophet Nathan confronted David over his sin with Bathsheba, he chose to tell a story rather than recite a commandment (and likely saved his own life in the process; see 2 Samuel 12). What biblical stories shape your beliefs? *(Use the whiteboard again here to record answers.)*

9. It's tempting, especially in times of crisis, to jump directly to practices. We want to fix the problem as we perceive it. Can you think of examples when a premature leap to rules and behaviors did more harm than good?

10. We tend to leap from beliefs directly to practice, but Paul addressed the Corinthians' attitudes first. He writes in 1 Corinthians 8:8-13,

> Food won't bring us close to God. We're not missing out if we don't eat, and we don't have any advantage if we do eat. But watch out or else this freedom of yours might be a problem for those who are weak. Suppose someone sees you (the person who has knowledge) eating in an idol's temple. Won't the person with a weak conscience be encouraged to eat the meat sacrificed to false gods? The weak brother or sister for whom Christ died is destroyed by your knowledge. You sin against Christ if you sin against your brothers and sisters and hurt their weak consciences this way. This is why, if food causes the downfall of my brother or sister, I won't eat meat ever again, or else I may cause my brother or sister to fall.

What sorts of attitudes prevail within your congregation? *(Write answers on whiteboard.)* If a guest visited your church, what attitudes would they encounter? *(Pay particular attention to any* actual *guests in the room or to relative newcomers to the church. These people will consistently have a perspective on the church's ethos that's much harder for long-term members to recognize.)* How would guests describe the spirit of your congregation? Are these attitudes consistent with your beliefs or contrary to them?

11. What are your church's ambitions for the next year? For the next five years? The next generation? The next century? *(Write answers on white-board.)* How do we reconcile holy ambition with the warning of James 4:13-15?

> Pay attention, you who say, "Today or tomorrow we will go to such-and-such a town. We will stay there a year, buying and selling, and making a profit." You don't really know about tomorrow. What is your life? You are a mist that appears for only a short while before it vanishes. Here's what you ought to say: "If the Lord wills, we will live and do this or that."

How do we manage appropriate ambition while holding on loosely to these goals?

12. Paul warns against "beating the air" like a futile boxer (1 Cor 9:26, NIV[12]). Are there any areas where you or your church are swinging at nothing? Have you fallen prey to misplaced ambition?

---

12. Scripture quotations marked NIV taken from The Holy Bible, New International Version, 2011.

# 2. Beliefs

> *Dear friends, I wanted very much to write to you concerning the salvation we share. Instead, I must write to urge you to fight for the faith delivered once and for all to God's holy people.*
>
> Jude 3

Vacation Bible School has gone wild. VBS began as a humble program to teach schoolchildren Scripture during the dog days of summer. Much has changed between 1894 and the current moment. The goal of Vacation Bible School is largely the same, but the methods create far more shock and awe. At VBS things tend to blow up, melt, fly away, ooze, flash, honk, and holler. Volunteer church artists produce set designs that shame local community theaters. Volunteers cry. Kids fall asleep in the midafternoon. VBS has become a wild week on the yearly congregational calendar.

In 2019 our congregation, First Baptist Church Waco, contracted with a recreation company to turn all the little children that Jesus loves into human pinballs. It was a VBS spectacle of the first order. We basically stuffed kids into gigantic, translucent, inflated rubber balls. We then proceeded to kick, roll, bounce, and throw the balls as if they did not have little children that Jesus loves inside of them. The kids loved it! Hindsight taught us, however, that we should have done this spectacle before the Kona Ice snow cone truck showed up. But hey, it was VBS! "Wow!" "This was great." "What are we going to do next year at VBS?" Little did we know as we finished those snow cones that next year we would hit a hard pause.

COVID-19 threw a muzzle on VBS in 2020. To be honest, COVID took a meat cleaver to the whole church calendar that year. We canceled most of what we had intended to do, and we radically altered the ministries that continued due to a force beyond our vision or control. Should we all wear gigantic, translucent, inflated rubber balls and do all the same stuff we had always done? We seriously considered and then nixed that notion. What would we do since we couldn't do what we had done before? Are we simply the sum of our practices, or is there more? Are we bound by what is seen, or are we held together by things unseen?

N. T. Wright says, "Theology is the backbone of a healthy church."[1] The church is endoskeletal, not exoskeletal. We are the body of Christ, not the body of a crawfish. The body needs the backbone. We see the need for good theology best in times of crisis. When the lines fall in pleasant places, we can daydream about VBS set design and a zillion other things that people see. Externals are important. Practices are valuable, even vital. When crisis comes, however, we have to find our spine.

## Working the Dough with Jude

Like the spine gives structure and strength to the body, flour gives structure and strength to a batch of dough. Pizza dough is made with flour, water, yeast, oil, salt, and sugar. Failing to give attention to Christian doctrine is like leaving the flour out of the dough. Our task is to work the whole batch of congregational dough, to blend the elements of soul culture. We begin with beliefs because they make the church the church. Our bedrock conviction that Jesus is Lord as revealed in Scripture identifies us as the church and not some other social organization. During our lived experience, we engage all five ingredients of soul culture simultaneously. This daily mixture of beliefs, attitudes, values, goals, and practices is precisely why it's necessary to pause, zoom out, and address beliefs conceptually prior to the other ingredients. This attention to beliefs is what Jude provided in the earliest years of Christian history. His work is a helpful guide for working the core beliefs of the church.

Jude wrote a scrappy little epistle, rallying the church to "fight for the faith delivered once and for all . . ." (Jude 3). Did you catch the word *the*? Our faith has real content, and that content is consequential. We also learn that the faith is often counterfeited.[2] Alternatives challenge it. Many of these counterfeits look and feel good. The *zeitgeist*, the spirit of this age, threatens to culture our congregations in place of the Holy Spirit. We can build our lives and churches on the content-rich faith that was delivered once and for all to God's holy people, or we can build them on scraps of ideas that form a social imaginary, our culturally created and usually unconscious assumptions about the deepest structures of reality and what's

1. N. T. Wright, *Paul: A Biography* (New York: HarperOne, 2018), 428–29.

2. See Trevin Wax, *Counterfeit Gospels: Rediscovering the Good News in a World of False Hope* (Chicago: Moody Publishers, 2011).

possible.[3] The counterfeits bore into our spine like cancer. As we work beliefs in the batch of dough, we need both construction and contention.

## Constructive Theology

When we say the faith has constructive content, we are talking about Christian doctrine. Jaroslav Pelikan defined doctrine as "What the church of Jesus Christ believes, teaches, and confesses on the basis of the Word of God."[4] Doctrine is the confessional proclamation at the heart of the church. It is the truth that God has placed in our midst through the grace of revelation. If we do not honor the reality that the faith is content-rich because there is a body of truth given to us by God, we are left with paltry substitutes. If we forget that the faith is content-rich, then the church becomes the Kiwanis Club with better music, the Rotary Club with softball and potlucks. If we neglect doctrine, the church becomes a sociological reality devoid of the life of God. Something stronger than the notion of being together must hold the church together. Community cannot be the basis of community. That notion is bankrupt.

The impulse to downplay doctrine has been a perennial temptation for the church. English novelist and playwright Dorothy Sayers challenged this tendency. As a close friend of G. K. Chesterton, C. S. Lewis, and several others in the literary group the Inklings, not to mention an accomplished author in her own right, Sayers appreciated the power of stories to sculpt our imagination. In 1938 she wrote a piece called *The Greatest Drama Ever Staged*. In it she said,

> Official Christianity, of late years, has been having what is known as "a bad press." We are constantly assured that the churches are empty because preachers insist too much on doctrine—"dull dogma," as people call it.

---

3. Charles Taylor coined the term "social imaginary" in his watershed work *A Secular Age* (Cambridge, MA: Belknap, 2007). Numerous others have borrowed and built on Taylor's social imaginary concept, most notably James K. A. Smith, *Desiring the Kingdom: Worship, Worldview, and Cultural Formation* (Grand Rapids, MI: Baker Academic: 2009); *How (Not) to Be Secular: Reading Charles Taylor* (Grand Rapids, MI: Eerdmans, 2014); and Carl R. Trueman, *The Rise and Triumph of the Modern Self: Cultural Amnesia, Expressive Individualism, and the Road to Sexual Revolution* (Wheaton, IL: Crossway, 2020).

4. Jaroslav Pelikan, *Reformation of Church and Dogma*, vol. 4 of The Christian Tradition: A History of the Development of Doctrine (Chicago: University of Chicago Press, 1983), 3.

> The fact is the precise opposite. It is the neglect of dogma that makes for dullness. The Christian faith is the most exciting drama that ever staggered the imagination of man—and the dogma is the drama.[5]

We are recipients of doctrines that dance.[6] Christian beliefs are dynamic and animating.

Jude wrote, "But you, dear friends, remember the words spoken beforehand by the apostles of our Lord Jesus Christ" (Jude 17). Jude lays out in this verse what Karl Barth would come to call the word of God in threefold sense.[7] First, Jesus Christ is the Word. Hebrews 1:1-2 says, "In the past, God spoke through the prophets to our ancestors in many times and many ways. In these final days, though, he spoke to us through a Son." Christ is the Word of God. He is the divine revelation.

We can also speak of Scripture as the word of God, the second of Barth's "threefold senses." Ephesians 2:20 reads, "As God's household, you are built on the foundation of the apostles and prophets with Christ Jesus himself as the cornerstone." The Bible is the book of Christ. The prophets and apostles witness to him. The prophets and apostles are like the cherubim on the ark of the covenant. They reach forward and backwards with Christ in the center. The red letters (that is, the words of Christ) of John 5:39 say, "Examine the scriptures, since you think that in them you have eternal life. They also testify about me." How amazing is that! Christ-exalting Scripture study needs to be a major part of every congregation's culture. It has been this way since the beginning.

In his excellent work *Destroyer of the Gods: Early Christian Distinctiveness in the Roman World*, Larry Hurtado describes Christianity as a "bookish" religion. He says, "This is not a new observation on my part. Other scholars also have referred to early Christian circles as 'constitutionally oriented to texts' and as 'textual communities' and have described the early Christian

---

5. Dorothy L. Sayers, *The Greatest Drama Ever Staged* (London: Hodder and Stoughton, 1938), 1.

6. See Robert Smith Jr., *Doctrine that Dances: Bringing Doctrinal Preaching and Teaching to Life* (Nashville, TN: B&H Academic, 2008).

7. Karl Barth, *The Doctrine of the Word of God*, vol. 1.2 of Church Dogmatics, ed. G. W. Bromiley and T. F. Torrance, trans. G. T. Thomson and Harold Knight (Edinburgh: T&T Clark: 1956), especially §22.1, "The Word of God and the Word of Man in Christian Preaching," 743–57.

movement collectively as one with 'texts at its very heart and soul.'"[8] The texts were at its heart because the church had a deep conviction that the texts have a heart and speak a living word.

The third sense in which we speak, along with Barth, of the word of God is the word as the faithful proclamation of the church. One of the most stunning verses in Scripture is Acts 4:31: "After they prayed, the place where they were gathered was shaken. They were all filled with the Holy Spirit and began speaking God's word with confidence." Notice a few things about this verse. The writer Luke says, "After they prayed . . . ." Acts 4:23-31 describes a congregational prayer meeting. The church believed in a God who tended to break in and do God things. One of our greatest needs is a firm conviction that God is God, and the church is not the star of its own show. Andrew Root brilliantly explores this theme in a series of books that focus on faithful ministry in this moment in time. In the volume titled *Churches and the Crisis of Decline: A Hopeful, Practical Ecclesiology for a Secular Age*, he writes, "*The church cannot produce its own life.* As a created thing, it cannot do so. Nothing created can produce its own life by its own will and energy. . . . [For] the church to live, its life must be seen as a gift from the Holy Spirit."[9]

God delights in gifts from the Holy Spirit. After the disciples prayed, "they were all filled with the Holy Spirit." As we work the dough of congregational soul culture, we need to learn to wait on the Spirit of God. Years ago, the pioneering Baptist ethicist T. B. Maston wrote, "We need to cultivate the art of tarrying until we are conscious of his presence, until we feel the touch of the divine Spirit. Our going into the world to witness for him by the spoken word and by the life we live will be effective to the degree that we have been 'clothed with power from on high.'"[10]

An infilling of the Spirit and waiting prayer led *all* the church to speak God's word with confidence. When a Spirit-filled church is faithful to proclaim God's word, then God's word "happens." God works in and through his church to amplify the testimony of Jesus. Doctrines that dance are Spirit-filled, confident proclamations of God's word. The New

---

8. Larry W. Hurtado, *Destroyer of the Gods: Early Christian Distinctiveness in the Roman World* (Waco, TX: Baylor University Press, 2008), 105–106.

9. Andrew Root, *Churches and the Crisis of Decline: A Hopeful, Practical Ecclesiology for a Secular Age* (Grand Rapids, MI: Baker Academic, 2022), 13 (emphasis original).

10. T. B. Maston, *Why Live the Christian Life?* (New Orleans: Insight Press, 1996), 60.

Testament sometimes refers to this as "the spirit of prophecy" (e.g., Rev 19:10). The faith says that the church is to be a Spirit-filled community of prophets, sharing the life of Christ with others and living by it for one another.

The priesthood of all believers is a cherished doctrine for many Christians. The doctrine is one of the great achievements of the Protestant Reformation. It recognizes and celebrates the privilege and responsibility of all Christians to enter God's presence with confidence through the high priesthood of Jesus, particularly for the sake of intercession on behalf of our sisters and brothers in the faith (Heb 4:14-16). The apostle Peter declared the church a holy, royal priesthood (1 Pet 2:5-9), fulfilling promises as old as Moses (Exod 19:6). The priesthood of all believers honors and exalts the individual but always does so *for the sake of others*. Too often the biblical picture of priestly sacrifice and service has devolved into a slogan for individual autonomy.

We can recover and strengthen this precious doctrine by adding its twin sister to the mix: the prophethood of all believers. The twentieth-century Baptist theologian H. Wheeler Robinson wrote, "Not only can we claim the priesthood of the believer, but we can claim the prophethood of the believer, for the task[s] of evangelism and missions belong to all of us."[11] The Spirit-inspired testimony of Jesus is indeed for the sake of the whole world. God has also elected to use the prophethood of the believer to encourage, console, and correct the church of Christ. The priesthood and prophethood of the believer reflect a biblical way of thinking and feeling born of an experimental knowledge of God.

Larry Hart places emphasis on the prophethood of all believers in the Luke/Acts narratives. It grew out of Moses's longing in Numbers 11:29.[12] If you haven't read Numbers 11 lately, you may want to pause and turn there now. Weary of manna, the Hebrews in the wilderness cry out for the leeks and onions of Egypt. Weary of the Hebrews' whining, Moses declares that he has had enough! He grows so discouraged that he asks the Lord, "If you're going to treat me like this, please kill me" (Num 11:15). God graciously offers an alternative solution, instructing Moses to summon

---

11. Quoted in Joel C. Gregory, "Impersonating a Priest," in *Distinctly Baptist: Proclaiming Identity in a New Generation*, ed. Brian C. Brewer (Valley Forge, PA: Judson Press, 2011), 46.

12. Larry D. Hart, *Truth Aflame: Theology for the Church in Renewal*, rev. ed. (Grand Rapids, MI: Zondervan, 2005), 398.

seventy elders to join him at the tent of meeting. There God places the Spirit on the seventy elders to assist Moses in leading the people.

Eldad and Medad, however, are late to the prayer meeting. (Pastors today might draw some encouragement that stragglers wandering late into the worship service is nothing new.) Even though these elders have tarried in the camp, "[yet] the Spirit also rested on them, and they prophesied in the camp" (Num 11:27, NIV). They do not fit the bill according to their neighbors, but God anoints them too, and they also prophesy. Joshua asks Moses if he wants to forbid them. Moses's response is amazing: "Are you jealous for my sake? If only all the LORD's people were prophets with the LORD placing his spirit on them!" (Num 11:29).

Joel later prophesies God's words in Joel 2:28, "After that I will pour out my spirit upon everyone; your sons and your daughters will prophesy, your old men will dream dreams, and your young men will see visions." This passage later becomes Peter's text for the first Christian sermon in the history of the world. It starts with the stunning line, "We aren't drunk." Peter then declares that Moses's dream and Joel's prophecy are taking shape in the streets of Jerusalem. Luke goes on to narrate the church's emergence as a Spirit-filled prophetic community. Spirit-driven proclamation was far from a one-time phenomenon. Two chapters later, Luke reports a prayer gathering following Peter and John's liberation from the hostile authorities. After prayer the Spirit manifests, "[they] were *all* filled with the Holy Spirit and began speaking God's word with confidence" (Acts 4:31, emphasis added).

This declaration of the word of God is the essence of biblical prophecy. It is not exclusively, nor even primarily, predictive (although it may be); instead, prophecy is proclamation of the good news. We depend on Spirit-enabled prophecy to apply God's word to continually changing circumstances. Hebrews tells us that "Jesus Christ is the same yesterday, today, and forever!" (13:8), but not much of anything else is. Peter prophetically reapplies an earlier word from the prophet Isaiah to remind us that "the grass dries up and its flower falls off, but the Lord's word endures forever" (1 Pet 1:24-25; cf. Isa 40:68) . . . but little else does. Nothing stays fixed. Because we live in such a shifting world, we rely on prophets to speak a consistent word to a new context time and time again.

Hart leans on Edward Schweizer and outlines the Lukan emphasis this way:

> (1) "[To prophesy] is for Luke quite central as *the* work of the Spirit. . . . The eschatological community is for Luke the community of the prophets."
> (2) "Luke thus shares with Judaism the view that the Spirit is essentially the Spirit of prophecy."
> (3) "The prophets are no longer isolated individuals.[13] All the members of the eschatological community are prophets."
> (4) "In the new age of salvation all members of the community rather than special individuals are bearers of the Spirit . . . ."[14]

He concludes, "Thus, to the Protestant paradigm of 'the priesthood of all believers' we can add the equally essential Lukan concept of 'the prophethood of all believers.'"[15]

The prophethood of *all* believers builds vital accountability into our shared work of prophecy. The apostle John warned the church to "[test] the spirits . . . because many false prophets have gone into the world" (1 John 4:1; cf. Deut 18:21-22). Not every spirit is the Holy Spirit, and not every word is a word from the Lord. Writing in Waco we are acutely aware of the peril of such false prophecy. Sharing the mantle of prophecy is a bulwark against this danger. The first test of prophecy, Barth's third sense of the word of God, is always its consistency with the first two senses, the written word and the Incarnate Word of Christ. After these plumb lines of Scripture and Jesus, the most rigorous system of checks and balances against perjured prophecy is the company of the prophets, the collective wisdom of the church endowed with the Spirit of Christ.

The threefold word of God nourishes the church's faith. God is revealed in Christ and witnessed to in the Scriptures. We grow in our faith by saturating our lives with the Scriptures. We can also seek a good God and ask for the infilling of the Holy Spirit. God's mercies are new every morning,

---

13. We would add that even within the Old Testament when charismatic gifting was more selective, the normative pattern seems to have been a community or "company" of prophets (e.g., 1 Kgs 20:35; 2 Kgs 2:3-15; 4:1, 38; 5:22; 6:1; 9:1). After a signal victory, the heroic prophet Elijah sank into despair and told God, "[The] Israelites have abandoned your covenant. They have torn down your altars, and they have murdered your prophets with the sword. I'm the only one left . . ." (1 Kgs 19:14). Truly it is not good for a human—even a prophet—to be alone. Among other mercies, the Lord commissions Elijah to anoint a successor as his protégé (19:16) and reassures him, "Yet I reserve seven thousand in Israel . . ." (1 Kgs 19:18, NIV).

14. Hart, *Truth Aflame*, 380.

15. Ibid.

and it's God's delight to give us the Spirit.[16] When the word and Spirit fill our lives, we overflow. What comes out are Spirit-animated words of life. These words enter the world through sermons and lessons but also in testimony, deliberation, hushed conversations, and sanctified small talk. Sometimes the most poignant moments of prophecy arise as friends interact with Christ in their midst and the Spirit transforms mundane chat into wonderful words of life. Dietrich Bonhoeffer reflected,

> God has put his Word into the mouth of men in order that it may be communicated to other men. When one person is struck by the Word, he speaks it to others. God has willed that we should seek and find His living Word in the witness of a brother, in the mouth of man. Therefore, the Christian needs another Christian who speaks God's Word to him.[17]

The words of the wise are like well-fixed nails. They build up the church. When this happens, dogma becomes drama and doctrines dance.

## Counterfeits

Jude wanted simply to write to a church and celebrate the constructive theology that is the faith. He said, "I wanted very much to write to you concerning the salvation we share" (v. 3). Most Christians share this desire to delight in our common salvation. Over the years a number of pastors, youth pastors, and theologians have suggested that if Christians knew the content of their faith well, they would be protected from counterfeits. One particular analogy made the rounds and was given a weight of authority when Millard Erickson repeated it.[18] The illustration goes something like this: Bank tellers and federal agents are trained to detect counterfeit money by studying only real currency. They know the real deal and can detect the phonies. The analogy is clear. Know the faith, and the counterfeits will reveal themselves.

This analogy bothered theologian Roger Olson. His irritation led him to a letter exchange with the federal government. Uncle Sam's representatives assured Dr. Olson that agents diligently studied counterfeiting techniques

---

16. See Luke 11:13.

17. Dietrich Bonhoeffer, *Life Together* (New York: HarperOne, 1978), 22–23.

18. Millard Erickson, *Christian Theology* (Grand Rapids, MI: Baker Academic, 2013), 15–16.

as well as legitimate currency.[19] Sometimes you must get to know the fakes. When we work the ingredient of beliefs into the congregational dough, we need to know the types of beliefs that do not belong in the bowl. Jude's desire was to be constructive, so he also had to be contentious.

Jude wanted to write one sort of letter but wound up writing another because of reports that he received. He heard that false teachers had infiltrated the church and were buttering up wavering people and winning them to a "gospel" contrary to the gospel of Christ. Their ingredients were disordered. The buttery enriched dough of a croissant has savory attraction, but it can't nourish in the same way over time as a hearty wheat loaf. So Jude proceeded to lay out the characteristics of the creeping religious counterfeit that opposed the faith. Creepy counterfeit religion has a soul culture too. It is made up of real ingredients like the authentic loaf of sincerity and truth. There is nothing new under the sun. Understanding the challenges faced by Jude's church heightens the probability that we will meet the challenge of the present moment.

Counterfeit faith often lacks an ethical dimension. Jude said that they turned the grace of God into license to sin (v. 4). One counterfeiting technique is to teach creation without corruption and affirmation without judgment. This type of thinking creeps into the love feasts and leaves stains. It is tempting, however, because it promises to relieve the pressure that comes from the ambient culture.

The current cultural moment is one dominated by expressive individualism, the exaltation of self-actualization as the greatest good. It is Nietzsche's day. Many people who have never read or even heard of his *Beyond Good and Evil* nevertheless sound like the philosopher's parrot because his ideas have carried the cultural day. They have become the water in which the church swims. The constant pressure to conform makes it difficult to flourish as the unique people of God. Paul warned of this pressure in Romans 12. J. B. Phillips paraphrased his words this way: "Don't let the world around you squeeze you into its own mould, but let God remould your minds from within."[20] A generation later Eugene Peterson updated Phillips's language with his own paraphrase: "Don't become so well-adjusted to your culture that you fit into it without even thinking.

---

19. Roger E. Olson, *The Story of Christian Theology* (Downers Grove, IL: IVP Academic, 1999), 20–21.

20. J. B. Phillips, *The New Testament in Modern English* (New York: MacMillan, 1958).

Instead, fix your attention on God."[21] Fitting in "without even thinking" is the culmination of a social imaginary, and it flourishes when being "well-adjusted" is the ideal. The only antidote is to "fix your attention on God," and to do so, faithful doctrine is crucial.

Counterfeit faith denies the only Lord Jesus Christ (Jude 4). Now this denial does not mean that a group of Christians infected by it will suddenly quit singing "Jesus Loves Me." It does mean that Jesus is recast, most often in the image of the counterfeiters. To do so is to transform Jesus into something less than Lord. The interlopers in Jude were diminishing Christ. Jude said that they followed the way of Cain and Balaam. In other words, they weren't all that innovative. Most, perhaps all, counterfeit faith is recycled. Jude's adversaries were not fresh thinkers. They followed old worn paths off the way. It did not work for Cain. It did not work for Balaam. It would not work for Jude's antagonists, and if we are tempted, we can be assured that it will not work for us either.

Jude used a delicious insult to describe the counterfeiters. He called them "waterless clouds" (Jude 12). We live in Texas. Drought is a real issue in our part of the world. Drought is damaging. It is costly. It can even be deadly. Longing for rain during a drought is deep and painful. From time to time, large clouds will roll in and hover low with promise. You can almost smell the rain; your mind tells you that you do. When those clouds ride the wind away without a drop, disappointment is overwhelming. The earth groans for the water of life. Doctrine matters because false doctrine promises life where there is none to be found.

Counterfeit faith is greedy. The antagonists in Jude were known to flatter people in order to acquire favors in return (Jude 11). Faith, for them, was a means to an end. The grand telos was self. If God is not God, then life is just a game of Hungry Hungry Hippos. In this classic tabletop game, bright plastic hippos gobble up marbles until the hungriest hippo wins. Our teenagers recently transformed the concept into a life-sized game. Pairs of students worked together. One student rolled on a mechanic's dolly into the play area and tried to trap pit balls beneath a 5-gallon bucket. Meanwhile, the other person used a rope to retract the dolly so that the pair could hoard their "hippo food" from the other teams. The game was a smash hit for Wednesday-night youth group, but it's a pitiful way to live. Greedy gobbling may be fine for a hippo, but it's far too hollow for a human being

---

21. Eugene H. Peterson, *The Message: The New Testament in Contemporary Language* (Colorado Springs, CO: NavPress, 1993).

made in the image and likeness of God. Nevertheless, false teaching is a massive business in the United States. Scores of talented people will tell you exactly what you want to hear . . . for a price. They promise to tell how to gobble the most marbles before time runs out, all the while pressing the levers to do gobbling of their own.

The most consistent characteristic of counterfeit faith is described in Jude 19: "Since they don't have the Spirit, they are worldly." N. T. Wright renders it this way: "They are living on the merely human level."[22] Many today assert that this is the only level there is. Philosopher Charles Taylor describes the day in which we are living as the secular age.[23] He says that the social imaginary, the way the world thinks, has created a scenario where we can imagine living without God. He calls this set of circumstances the immanent frame. Think of it as an impenetrable dome insulating our material lives from outside realities, the spiritual version of Tony Stark's desire to build a "suit of iron" around the world. We imagine ourselves safe from magic, karma, and Santeria, but we buy our security at the price of a living connection with God. For the church, this means that even though we continue to use the language of faith, often we believe, "If it's going to be, it's up to me." In this frame of vision, we feel free to choose our own adventures. We live on a "merely human" plane, devoid of the Spirit. The consequences of this disenchanted life can be quite bleak.

In *The Wizard of Oz*, there is a good witch and a wicked witch. They are both witches, but they have different publicists. There is a sweet version and a sour version of counterfeit religion in the secular age. The sweet version has an absent but affirming God. The sour one squarely accepts the terms of God's demise.

Michael Gungor gives us an example of the sweet version. He once tweeted, "Heaven is not a place where you are made perfect after you die. Heaven is the realization that you're already perfect as you are now."[24] That sounds lovely until you realize it is utterly depressing. We would be doomed to call many evil things good in this scenario. This type of idea has been around for quite a long time. C. S. Lewis confronted it in *Mere*

---

22. *The Bible for Everyone*, trans. John Goldingay and Tom Wright (London: SPCK, 2018).

23. Taylor, *Secular Age*.

24. Michael Gungor (@michaelgungor), "Heaven is not a place . . . ," Twitter, May 22, 2020, https://twitter.com/michaelgungor/status/1264041473986551808?lang=en.

*Christianity*. He wrote, "Confronted with a cancer or a slum the Pantheist can say, 'If you could only see it from the divine point of view, you could realise that this also is God.' The Christian replies, 'Don't talk damned nonsense.'"[25] He included an asterisk with a note explaining that he was not using "damned" in a frivolous way, as one radio listener had complained he was doing. Instead, "I mean exactly what I say—nonsense that is *damned* is under God's curse, and will (apart from God's grace) lead those who believe it to eternal death."[26]

The creative content of Christian faith is bold to call counterfeits nonsense. Christianity says that God made the world. God made space and time, heat and cold, colors and taste, animals and vegetables. The faith also says a great many things have gone wrong in this world because of sin and rebellion, and God is bent on setting them right. The word of God confronts us with both judgment and grace because God is love. The good witch in the evening gown may show up and say, "All is well." The faith responds, "That's damned nonsense." Doctrine constructs, but it also contends.

The sour version of counterfeit thinking in the secular age comes to us from nihilism and absurdism. Jean-Paul Sartre famously said, "Everything is indeed permitted if God does not exist, and man is in consequence forlorn, for he cannot find anything to depend upon either within or outside himself. He discovers forthwith, that he is without excuse."[27] Authenticity becomes holiness, and we move past good and evil.[28] Popular culture weaves these notions into television dialogue and song lyrics. *Yellowstone*'s Beth Dutton is Nietzsche's apostle. The show is one of the most popular on television. Its philosophy partly drives its appeal. Many now think in Nietzschean ways—characterized by radical individualism, tribalism, and the rejection of truth in favor of raw personal power.

The church isn't immune from sour counterfeits either. The flour of belief must mix rightly with the other ingredients: attitudes, values, goals, and practices. Cold ideological assent to a doctrinal statement or catechism

---

25. C. S. Lewis, *Mere Christianity* (New York: HarperCollins, 2001), 37.

26. Ibid.

27. Jean-Paul Sartre, "Existentialism Is a Humanism," in *Existentialism from Dostoyevsky to Sartre*, ed. Walter Kaufmann (New York: Meridian, 1956), available online at https://www.marxists.org/reference/archive/sartre/works/exist/sartre.htm.

28. See Friedrich Nietzsche, *Beyond Good and Evil: On the Genealogy of Morality*, trans. Adrian Del Caro (Stanford, CA: Stanford University Press, 2014).

isn't enough. Paul warned, "If I have the gift of prophecy and I know all mysteries and everything else, and if I have such complete faith that I can move mountains but I don't have love, I'm nothing" (1 Cor 13:2). A quick glance at Christian Twitter reveals the danger when brains and bodies run rampant without heart. Becoming righteous is more than being "right."

The Joker is burning down the city. When we deny God and deny hope, this despair is always the last scene. Doctrine matters. To borrow a line from Richard M. Weaver, "Ideas have consequences."[29] The faith has rich content, so rich that it is often counterfeited. Christian thinking is constructive, but it also contends. We need to remember both of these dimensions of the faith as we work the ingredient of beliefs into our congregation's soul culture.

## Constructive Theology Revisited

Jude began his epistle declaring his desire to celebrate the salvation he shared with the church. He shifted to confront the lifeless counterfeit faith that had slipped into the congregation, damaging the soul culture of God's people. At the end of his little letter, he returned to the faith and its constructive power. Jude wrote,

> But you, dear friends: build each other up on the foundation of your most holy faith, pray in the Holy Spirit, keep each other in the love of God, wait for the mercy of our Lord Jesus Christ, who will give you eternal life. Have mercy on those who doubt. Save some by snatching them from the fire. Fearing God, have mercy on some, hating even the clothing contaminated by their sinful urges. (Jude 20–23)

We can build ourselves up in the faith by praying in the Holy Spirit. One of the best ways to pray in the Spirit is to pray the prayer given to us by the Lord. When we say to God, "your kingdom come, your will be done, on earth as it is in heaven" (Matt 6:10, NIV) and wait, God gives us the Holy Spirit. God's good future breaks in. We construct ourselves in faith by remembering we are not mere mortals.

The faith says we are called to be a Spirit-filled community of prophets, breathing in and out the word of God. When we work beliefs into the soul culture, we primarily do that by facilitating getting the word in and out of

29. Richard M. Weaver, *Ideas Have Consequences* (Chicago: University of Chicago Press, 2013).

our people. There are some basic elements of this process that we need to teach and model. We can encourage daily Bible reading. We need a plan to read Scripture consistently. Some plans have been around for generations. Robert Murray M'Cheyne's reading plan has blessed millions and is easily available online. Dietrich Bonhoeffer led his underground seminary to use the Daily Text published by the Moravian Church. This reading plan ministry is still ongoing, and it helps scores of Christians get the word into their lives. More recent projects like Robby Gallaty's Bible Reading Plan for Busy Believers continues the tradition of helping Christians meet God in the Bible. Digital tools like the Bible Project and the Bible Recap Podcast make reading and hearing the word easier than ever. We simply need to read the Bible if we are going to grow up in the faith.

We can lead the church to memorize small portions of Scripture and meditate on those words during the day. We can sing and pray the word. We can give critical reflections to worship elements and make sure they are rooted in the constructive content of the faith. We can study the word in small groups with attention to curricula, scope, and sequence. The Bible should be the primary text for each group, cradle to grave. Everything else is a tool to aid in understanding and application. Classes and groups are good environments to nurture the voice of the church. The word arrives, and it's a safe place for folks to attempt to share a word of testimony, encouragement, correction, or comfort. Living things breathe in and breathe out. Living congregations inhale and exhale the word of God.

The faith says we are an "each other" community. We are to keep each other in the love of God. We are to have mercy for the doubters. Church should be a place of vibrant faith for those who struggle with faith. We are a people of hope. We don't have to look at the mess and try to convince ourselves this life is as good as it gets. We wait for the mercy of Jesus Christ who *will* give us eternal life. Beliefs matter. Doctrine dances. We cannot be the people God wants us to be without giving attention to the faith delivered once and for all to God's holy people.

You would not attempt to make a pizza without flour. That's nonsense. Many churches attempt to build a platform in a community without giving attention to doctrine. This neglect leaves us immature and vulnerable. Beliefs matter, and ideas have consequences. Construct your life through the faith once and for all given to us. Contend for it with mercy and grace.

Chapter 2

# Beliefs

### Questions for Further Reflection

1. Read the brief letter of Jude. Verse 3 describes "*the* faith delivered once and for all." How would you summarize this faith in a few sentences? In other words, what do you believe?

2. Twentieth-century theologian Karl Barth wrote about the "threefold sense of the Word of God." Make a few notes about the significance of each of the three senses of the word to your beliefs.

- Jesus Christ the Word (John 1:14):

- Scripture as the Word of God:

- The church's faithful proclamation as the Word:

How do these three forms of the Word relate to one another?

3. Songs are a vital part of the church's faithful proclamation. The words that we sing together in worship teach and reinforce many of our deepest beliefs from earliest childhood through the last days of life. What songs of the church have particularly formed your beliefs?

4. Many Christians cherish the doctrine of the priesthood of all believers. Although it's sometimes caricatured into a slogan for radical individualism, a biblical understanding of priesthood recognizes and celebrates the privilege *and the responsibility* of all Christians to enter God's presence and intercede *for the sake of others.*

Most of us are less familiar with the prophethood of all believers, but it is likewise a promise running throughout Scripture. Moses cried out, "If only all the LORD's people were prophets with the LORD placing his spirit on them!" (Num 11:29). Joel prophesied the fulfillment of this plea when he foresaw, "After that I will pour out my spirit upon everyone; your sons and your daughters will prophesy" (Joel 2:28), and Peter took up this word as his text for the first Christian sermon in Acts 2. The essence of biblical prophecy is to declare the word of God. Do you consider yourself a prophet? In what ways can you declare the word of God this week?

5. Jude also warned the church about counterfeit alternatives to the gospel. These phony imitations
- Turn grace into license to sin
- Deny the exclusive Lordship of Jesus
- Reinforce greed
- Reduce reality to "the merely human level"

How do you see these counterfeits at work around you? Which form of counterfeit is most alluring and most dangerous to you personally?

# Chapter 2: Beliefs

## *Group Discussion Guide*

1. Does your church or ministry have a confession or statement of faith? What must someone believe in order to join or to partner with you?

*If you have a written statement, provide copies for everyone and spend some time doing a careful reading of the text, phrase by phrase. Encourage reflection on why particular beliefs are emphasized and expressed in the specific words chosen.*

*If your church or ministry does not have a written statement, reflect on why. If you were to adopt such a statement, what would you include?*

2. Confessions of shared, communal faith are embedded throughout the Bible:

- **Exodus 34:6-7**

"The LORD! The LORD! a God who is compassionate and merciful, very patient, full of great loyalty and faithfulness, showing great loyalty to a thousand generations, forgiving every kind of sin and rebellion, yet by no means clearing the guilty, punishing for their parents' sins their children and their grandchildren, as well as the third and the fourth generation."

- **Deuteronomy 6:4**

"Israel, listen! Our God is the LORD! Only the LORD!"

- **Matthew 16:16**

"You are the Christ, the Son of the living God."

- **John 11:27**

"I believe that you are the Christ, God's Son, the one who is coming into the world."

- **Philippians 2:5-11**

"Adopt the attitude that was in Christ Jesus: Though he was in the form of God, he did not consider being equal with God something to exploit. But he emptied himself by taking the form of a slave and by becoming like human beings. When he found himself in the form of a human, he humbled himself by becoming obedient to the point of death, even death on a cross. Therefore, God highly honored him and gave him a name above all names, so that at the name of Jesus everyone in heaven, on earth, and under the earth might bow and every tongue confess that Jesus Christ is Lord, to the glory of God the Father."

- **2 Timothy 2:11-13**

"This saying is reliable: 'If we have died together, we will also live together. If we endure, we will also rule together. If we deny him, he will also deny us. If we are disloyal, he stays faithful' because he can't be anything else than what he is."

*Divide into groups and assign each one a biblical text. What stands out about these declarations of belief? Spend 5 to 10 minutes in small group discussion and then return and share observations with the entire group.*

3. In the same small groups, take a look at some of the historic statements of belief from various Christian traditions (all of the ones below are readily available online):
    - The Apostles' Creed
    - The Nicene Creed
    - The Westminster Confession
    - The Thirty-Nine Articles
    - The Baptist Faith and Message

Does your church or denomination subscribe to one or more of these statements? Why or why not? What are the benefits of a shared statement of belief? Are there any corresponding dangers?

4. Twentieth-century theologian Karl Barth wrote about the "threefold sense of the Word of God": Jesus Christ the Word, Scripture as the Word of God, and the church's faithful proclamation as the word. How do these three authorities relate to one another?

5. What's the difference between a prophet and a priest? Brainstorm some contrasting traits and responsibilities for each one and record on a whiteboard or flip chart:

| Prophet | Priest |
| --- | --- |
| | |

6. Many Christians cherish the doctrine of the priesthood of all believers, but the prophethood of all believers receives much less attention (despite passages like Numbers 11:29; Joel 2:28; and Acts 2). What are the opportunities of recovering the prophethood of all believers? Are there any corresponding risks or challenges?

7. Our beliefs include settled, core convictions of the gospel (like the Lordship of the risen Jesus), doctrines that distinguish congregations and denominations within the church (like believers' baptism), and interpretations that mature Christians within the same congregation might differ over (like the precise sequence of events leading to Christ's return). What are some other examples of beliefs in each of these categories? *(Use the whiteboard to record answers in the chart.)* How do we distinguish between their relative priority?

| Core Gospel Convictions | Distinctive Doctrines | Varied Interpretations |
| --- | --- | --- |
| | | |

8. What counterfeits to the gospel have you encountered? *(Record answers on whiteboard.)* How do you recognize them? How do you respond (both personally and as a prophet for others)?

# 3. Attitudes

> *Therefore if there is any encouragement in Christ, any comfort in love, any sharing in the Spirit, any sympathy, complete my joy by thinking the same way, having the same love, being united, and agreeing with each other. Don't do anything for selfish purposes, but with humility think of others as better than yourselves. Instead of each person watching out for their own good, watch out for what is better for others.* ***Adopt the attitude that was in Christ Jesus.***
>
> **Philippians 2:1-5 (emphasis added)**

Jesus was funny. We often miss his humor when we read Scripture with adult eyes and an unsanctified seriousness. I think one place where we swing and miss in this way is the story that Matthew recorded in Matthew 16:5-12.

Jesus and the disciples crossed over a lake by boat. When they docked on the other side, the fellas made a discovery: ". . . they had forgotten to bring bread" (Matt 16:5). We all know how it feels to pull into the parking lot of the Motel 6 after a long journey and suddenly remember that a key item is not in the cartop carrier but rather sitting on the kitchen counter 1,043 miles away. Well, maybe you claim not to know this feeling, but chances are that someone you love probably does. Leaving things behind on a trip induces stress. It births many hassles. It causes embarrassment, blame, and normally a pretty good fight. Into this churning water, Jesus tossed the comment, "Watch out and be on your guard for the yeast of the Pharisees and Sadducees" (16:6).

The disciples started to whisper among themselves: "He knows!!! We better own up about forgetting the buns." Here's how Matthew records it: "They discussed this among themselves and said, 'We didn't bring any bread'" (16:7). Jesus responded as their rabbi and leader but also as their friend. I hear a bit of good-natured ribbing bust out in verses 8-11:

> "You people of weak faith! Why are you discussing among yourselves the fact that you don't have any bread? Don't you understand yet? Don't you remember the five loaves that fed the five thousand and how many baskets of leftovers we gathered? And the seven loaves that fed the four thousand and how many large baskets of leftovers you gathered? Don't you know that I wasn't talking about bread? But be on your guard for the yeast of the Pharisees and Sadducees."

Jesus's tone with his disciple-friends reminds me of a line from the film *The Sandlot*: "Come on. You're killing me, Smalls." He wasn't taking about bread; he was talking about bread!

They got it. Verse 12 makes it clear. They understood that he wasn't telling them to be on their guard for yeast used in making bread. No, he was telling them to watch out for the teaching of the Pharisees and Sadducees. In Jesus's world, teaching was not just a list of doctrinal statements. It was a total way of life. The yeast of the Pharisees and Sadducees was a metaphor for their entire way of living. Jesus warned his disciples to reject not only their doctrine but also their attitudes, values, goals, and practices. The Pharisees and Sadducees had a form of godliness but missed the life found in the kingdom message that Jesus preached and shaped among his people.

The disciples were gradually getting the message. What goes into the dough makes the loaf. Jesus wanted their loaf to be made of the right ingredients. He wanted them to beware of toxic alternatives and make bread with only the good stuff. He wants the same for us as well. We explored the ingredient called beliefs in our last chapter. We now turn to the importance of attitude.

## The Power of Attitude

The great American philosopher Jerry Jeff Walker once sang, "Life is mostly attitude and timing."[1] Since a good sense of timing is almost completely dependent on attitude, he could have sung, "Life is mostly attitude," but that would have probably fouled up the rhyme. Jerry Jeff was using hyperbolic simplicity to say that attitude is important. Scripture teaches the same lesson.

Our staff at First Baptist Church Waco received a wonderful reminder of the importance of attitude a few years ago during our annual Christmas

---

1. Jerry Jeff Walker, "Singin' the Dinosaur Blues," by Steven Fromholz, recorded 1992, track 3 on *Hill Country Rain*, 1992.

party when we snuck a surprise guest into Baylor University's McLane Stadium. Grant Teaff is a legendary football coach. He has more wins than any other coach in Baylor program history. He won the American Football Coaches Association Coach of the Year Award, the Eddie Robinson Coach of the Year Award, and the Amos Alonzo Stagg Award. Coach Teaff belongs to the College Football Hall of Fame and has a statue on campus. The man is a walking graven image. He is also a wise and humble deacon at First Baptist Waco and an amazing encourager. He was a life coach before that was a thing.

After our Christmas gift exchange, stadium personnel led the church staff from the Baylor Club to the home locker room. When we all got settled, Coach Teaff walked into the room, leaned on his cane, and summoned his coaching voice: "Okay team, listen up." He went on to give us a good old-fashioned pregame talk about attitude. Here we were, a motley collection of ministers, custodians, and administrative assistants, and when he was done, we were ready to tackle the Texas Longhorns. We were convinced that attitude matters. He made us believe.

Coach Teaff's talk on attitude is part of his life message. He once told an assembly of coaches,

> I said to my players and I said to those that would listen to me, "What I do every day is set my attitude." People say, "Why do you always have a positive attitude, and you're always on the go and you're always doing something?" I said, "Because it is self-imposed." A positive attitude is self-imposed. Every morning when I get up, I look into the mirror and say, "I'm only one, but I am one. I can't do everything, but I can do something. That which I ought to do, by God's grace, I will do." I'm like Pavlov's dog. Saying it right now makes the hairs stand up on the back of my head, because it triggers within me . . . .[2]

Coach Teaff was modeling the power of attitude and how to take responsibility for it. He was standing on biblical ground as he did so. David encouraged himself in the Lord during a time of severe trial. First Samuel 30:6 reads, "David was in deep trouble because the troops were talking about stoning him. Each of the soldiers was deeply distressed about their sons and daughters. But David found strength in the LORD his God." He

---

2. Grant Teaff, "Positive Attitude," American Football Coaches Association, Facebook video, posted September 8, 2016, https://www.facebook.com/WeAreAFCA/videos/1057487401013232/.

encouraged himself in God. This theme strikes a chord when it is preached, taught, and modeled in the church because we intuit how important it is.

Charles Swindoll is in his late eighties and still preaches two services a Sunday at Stonebriar Community Church in suburban Dallas. His most famous message is his sermon on attitude. It went viral back in the days when the only things that did so were actual viruses. The message became so popular that when Swindoll's daughter took a summer job at Nordstrom, she was surprised to find his word on attitude in the company's training manual. Businesses used it, and so did the military. Here's what Swindoll said:

> The longer I live, the more I realize the impact of attitude on life. Attitude, to me, is more important than facts. It is more important than the past, than education, than money, than circumstances, than failures, than successes, than what other people think or say or do. It is more important than appearance, giftedness, or skill. It will make or break a company . . . a church . . . a home. The remarkable thing is we have a choice every day regarding the attitude we will embrace for that day. We cannot change the inevitable. The only thing we can do is play on the one string we have, and that is our attitude. I am convinced that life is 10% what happens to me, and 90% how I react to it. And so it is with you . . . we are in charge of our Attitudes.[3]

And our attitudes are contagious. When we set our attitude, we can positively impact our family, church, or organization.

David Bolin retired after years of faithful service as First Baptist Waco's minister of music. David and his wife Julie relocated to Dallas and attend Stonebriar Community Church. We recently asked him about the impact of attitude in that congregation led by Swindoll. He said, "Years ago in Irving, Texas, I was at a church staff lunch with Jess Moody. The one thing from that conversation I remember is him saying, 'The pastor of the church is the mood maker.' So true. The warm heart comes through in Swindoll's preaching, and Stonebriar is a happy place because of it." We were pleased to discover that Swindoll continues to concretize his famous attitude sermon in Frisco, Texas. When leaders learn to encourage themselves in the Lord, the whole church benefits.

---

3. Charles Swindoll, "Attitude," Brigham Young University, 2007, available at https://womensconference.byu.edu/sites/womensconference.ce.byu.edu/files/25b_3.pdf.

Jess Moody would know. He lived that way too. We once heard music minister O. D. Hall speak at the Alleluia Worship Conference at Baylor. Hall served alongside Moody for decades. Moody would preach, and Hall would lead the music. Hall said of Moody, "When Jess entered a room, he filled it with laughing gas. Everyone got comfortable." This comment came in response to another worship leader saying that the pastor he served alongside sucked all the oxygen out of the room and made everyone tense whenever he walked in. Attitude is powerful. It creates a mood throughout the church, and that mood goes a long way in shaping a congregation's soul culture. We need to take charge of it and treat it with respect.

Lest you think we are championing some former-Marine, preacher-coach-talk, Texas Stoicism, recall that Scripture commands us to embrace the attitude of Christ for the sake of the church and our collective witness in the world. Attitude is a Christian idea.

## The Attitude of Christ

Paul encouraged the church at Philippi, "Adopt the attitude that was in Christ Jesus" (Phil 2:5). He was addressing a church that he dearly loved. God's people in Jesus Christ in Philippi believed the right things and were doing many of the right things. Part of the reason that Paul was writing them was to thank them for their partnership in the gospel. The problem the apostle felt obliged to address was the same one that Gordon Fee diagnosed as the challenge in Corinth: "The problem is primarily attitudinal."[4] The attitudes of two of the church's primary leaders had soured toward one another (see Phil 4:2-3). They had to get their attitudes right because attitude had become the primary problem in the congregation. How often this is the case! Many times, it seems churches and Christian organizations check the right boxes when it comes to beliefs, values, goals, and practices, but something still remains off, rendering the soul culture less than Christlike. Quite often the challenge is attitudinal.

The epistle to the Philippians is a training manual on resetting your attitude. If we understand what the attitude of Christ looks like, then we stand a better chance of cultivating it and spreading it to others. Paul outlines at least four marks of Christlike attitude in the letter: joy, gratitude, humility, and hope.

---

4. Gordon D. Fee, *The First Epistle to the Corinthians*, rev. ed., NICNT (Grand Rapids, MI: Eerdmans, 2014), 401.

## *Joy*

Philippians is known as the book of joy. It is a letter filled with and partially about joy. The first mention of joy is in 1:4: "I'm thankful for all of you every time I pray, and it's always a prayer full of joy." What a statement. If someone said that to you and you had the slightest notion that they were telling you the truth, it would encourage you. When Paul began to address toxic attitudes in the church and exhorted the Philippians to adopt the attitude of Christ, he said that doing so would "complete [his] joy" (Phil 2:2). Christlike attitude induces joy!

Jesus was a man of joy. While it is true that Jesus lived out the messianic imagery of Isaiah 53 as a man of sorrows, he was also a man of joy. These two realities were like a woven leather belt that encircled his life. The dialectic of sorrow and joy marks his churches. When Dietrich Bonhoeffer encountered the soul culture at Harlem's Abyssinian Baptist Church, he noted that their worship welded "reserved melancholy and eruptive joy."[5] Joy provides the strength necessary to carry out the assignment that God entrusts to us.

Nehemiah 8 provides a great example of the high and holy task of culturing a community of faith. All of Israel gathered to hear the word of the Lord. Ezra the priest brought the instruction. The sense of it was given to the people. They came to understand key biblical concepts. This labor in doctrine led into a rocking fellowship. Nehemiah 8:10 says, "Go, eat rich food, and drink something sweet . . . and send portions of this to any who have nothing ready! This day is holy to our LORD. Don't be sad, because the joy from the LORD is your strength!" So what did they do? "Then all of the people went to eat and to drink, to send portions, and to have a great celebration, because they understood what had been said to them" (Neh 8:12). The word of God and the people of God are designed to spark joy because God has ordained that joy is strength.

Jesus's joy sustained him as he went to the cross. Hebrews 12:1-2 contains some of the most stunning words in the entire corpus of Scripture. The text says,

> So then, with endurance, let's also run the race that is laid out in front of us, since we have such a great cloud of witnesses surrounding us. Let's throw off any extra baggage, get rid of the sin that trips us up, and fix

---

5. Quoted by Reggie L. Williams, *Bonhoeffer's Black Jesus: Harlem Renaissance Theology and an Ethic of Resistance*, rev. ed. (Waco, TX: Baylor University Press, 2021), 80.

> our eyes on Jesus, faith's pioneer and perfecter. He endured the cross, ignoring the shame, *for the sake of the joy that was laid out in front of him,* and sat down at the right side of God's throne [emphasis added].

Joy is a mark of a Christlike attitude. It is a strength and a motivating goal. We can build a culture of "J.O.Y."

The Baylor men's basketball team won the NCAA National Championship for the 2020–2021 season. Coach Scott Drew assembled the team from the most unlikely places and led them to believe in things larger than themselves. Drew is a sincere and winsome follower of Christ. He takes advantage of coaching at a Christian school to cultivate a distinctly Christlike culture for his team. He calls it the Culture of J.O.Y. Everyone can readily see that Drew's teams are joyfully exuberant. What one doesn't see as easily is how they pursue that joy. They don't chase joy for the sake of joy. They cultivate joy by giving descending priority to Jesus, Others, and You.[6] This model comes straight from Philippians, and as Drew has demonstrated, it still works mightily. Joy can be concretized on a Christian basketball team, in a congregation, in a family, and in your life.

## *Gratitude*

There are few things quite as powerful as an attitude of gratitude. Paul links joy and gratitude together in Philippians 4:4-6: "Be glad in the Lord always! Again I say, be glad! Let your gentleness show in your treatment of all people. The Lord is near. Don't be anxious about anything; rather, bring up all of your requests to God in your prayers and petitions, *along with giving thanks*" (emphasis added). Joy, faith, and gratitude battle the demon of anxiety, strengthen our souls, and nourish our churches' soul culture.

In culturing gratitude, we need to be aware that an attitude of entitlement is gratitude's sworn enemy. Philippians 2:3 says, "Do nothing out of selfish ambition or vain conceit" (NIV). An attitude of vain conceit, entitlement, is both toxic and as common as table salt. It strips us of joy and pollutes our congregations.

We were once interacting with one of our community's wealthiest citizens. He was making overtures about connecting with our church after being out of fellowship with any church since the 1970s. The reason he gave us for not worshiping with a community of fellow believers was jaw

---

6. See Scott Drew with Don Yaeger, *The Road to J.O.Y.: Leading with Faith, Living with Purpose, Leaving a Legacy* (Nashville, TN: Thomas Nelson, 2022).

dropping: "When it comes down to it, I'm just really hard to please." And we wonder why we are not happy. There are a number of Christians who believe deep down that God is lucky to have them. They have a Burger King theology. They want both God and church to say, "Have it your way." Tim Keller describes these folks as "middle-class in spirit."[7] The poverty of spirit that Jesus called blessed forsakes entitlement and receives life as gift.

In the place of entitlement, genuine gratitude creates what the old Pietists called gravitas. It is a way of life, a Christlike attitude, that was attractive to others. Gravitas is substantial and weighty, solid and secure. Gravitas gives off the fragrance of Christ. It is salt that makes others thirsty for God.

In the preface to his book *Diary of a Pastor's Soul*, Princeton Theological Seminary President Craig Barnes describes gravitas this way:

> No one is born with gravitas, and it's not exactly a spiritual gift. It comes as a result of good responses to hurts, blessings, failures, achievement, boredom, and obligations, all of which are surrendered to our Creator. Some who have the exact same experiences turn instead to cynicism. But souls with gravitas somehow choose to receive their lives, such as they are, with gratitude.[8]

Souls and soul cultures with gravitas have an attitude of gratitude.

## *Humility*

The most jarring mark of the attitude of Christ is humility. What should startle us is not that we are summoned to humility but that the biblical God is genuinely and truly humble. Karl Barth wrote, "God is not proud. In His high majesty He is humble."[9] We worship along with Paul and the Philippian believers as recorded in Philippians 2:6-11, where Paul breaks into song and lines the lyrics of an ancient Christ hymn. The poetry flows, and the Philippians recall Christ's world-changing humility. Paul

---

7. Timothy Keller, *Generous Justice: How God's Grace Makes Us Just* (New York: Penguin Books, 2012), 102.

8. M. Craig Barnes, *Diary of a Pastor's Soul: The Holy Moments in a Life of Ministry* (Grand Rapids, MI: Brazos Press, 2020), 13.

9. Karl Barth, *The Doctrine of Reconciliation*, vol. 4.1 of Church Dogmatics, ed. G. W. Bromiley and T. F. Torrance, trans. G. T. Thomson and Harold Knight (Edinburgh: Bloomsbury T&T Clark, 2004), 159.

admonished them, "Adopt the attitude that was in Jesus Christ" (Phil 2:5). Some translations render the call like this: "Have this *mind* among yourselves, which is yours in Christ Jesus" (Phil 2:5, ESV, emphasis added).[10] *Mind* is a helpful wording. It puts a bit of a handle on the attitude of Christ.

Quaker Philosopher Elton Trueblood had a dynamic understanding of the mind of Christ and what it would take to allow it to dwell in us. In 1969 Trueblood wrote a book titled *A Place to Stand: A Practical Guide to Christian Faith as a Solid Point from which to Operate in Contemporary Living*. That's got to be one of the great Christian book titles of the 1960s. In this work Trueblood wrote,

> The Christian who uses the phrase "the mind of Christ" is not using language in the same way as if he were to speak of the mind of Plato or Marx. We know something of the minds of these men because we can read what they wrote, but we mean something different in reference to Christ. We mean that Christ can be in *us*, that His very mentality comes to dominate ours. "Do you not realize," asks Paul, "that Jesus Christ is in you?" (II Cor. 13:5). Shocking as it sounds, it is really possible for a finite man, as he responds to Christ's call to have a measure of the spirit of Christ. The central purpose of the gospel is that Christ may be formed in *us* (Gal. 4:19) and that He may dwell in our hearts (Eph. 3:17).[11]

Adopting the attitude of Christ's humility is not an adventure in trying really, really hard to be like Jesus. It is the Holy Spirit's inside job. God works in us both to will and do the humble attitude of Jesus (see Phil 2:13). As we come to God for the life-giving milk of the word, his Spirit indwells us and gives us the mind of Christ. This spiritual dynamic may be what C. S. Lewis had in mind when he wrote of Deep Magic.[12]

We once saw a sign and wonder in person. One of our congregants manifested the mind of Christ when his own mind was all but gone. Brent Froberg was a brilliant man. He had a long career as a university professor.

---

10. Scripture quotations marked "ESV" are from The ESV Bible (The Holy Bible, English Standard Version), copyright 2001 by Crossway, a publishing ministry of Good News Publishers.

11. Elton Trueblood, *A Place to Stand: A Practical Guide to Christian Faith as a Solid Point from which to Operate in Contemporary Living* (New York: Harper and Row, 1969), 50.

12. See C. S. Lewis, *The Lion, the Witch, and the Wardrobe* (New York: Harper Collins, 2019).

He taught classics, including Greek and Latin. He was a sharp guy. Dr. Froberg had a show on the local public radio station called "A Word about Words." He would sit behind a microphone and in a stereotypical public radio voice trace the etymology of a common word. It was riveting radio, I promise.

Brent was also a humble and kind servant of Jesus. He was the VBS volunteer in the bow tie. He fed the hungry and taught the word and loved his wife like Christ loves the church. In the final weeks of his life, his mind grew dim. We visited him in a care facility near the end. We asked, "Brent, how's your day been?" He gave a detailed account of showing up at the church to help with a cleanup day. We almost believed him, even though we were certain he had not left his room in months. It was a kindness. When his mind was nearly gone, the mind of Christ was still there, serving, encouraging, loving, and living.

## *Hope*

Hope is life. We need it more than oxygen. Jürgen Moltmann once said, "[L]iving without hope is like no longer living. Hell is hopelessness . . . ."[13] The Christ hymn pivots sharply from humility to hope in Philippians 2:9-11: "Therefore, God highly honored him and gave him a name above all names, so that at the name of Jesus everyone in heaven, on earth, and under the earth might bow and every tongue confess that Jesus Christ is Lord, to the glory of God the Father." The cross led to the crown. Christ ignored the shame for the joy set before him. Our hope is built on nothing less than his hope.

It is important for us to note that adopting an attitude of Christlike hope requires us to view life as a two-tiered reality. There is both penultimate and ultimate hope, hope for now and for later. The full Serenity Prayer written by theologian Reinhold Niebuhr captures these two types of hope. Most of us know the first part, the part made famous by Alcoholics Anonymous: "God, grant me the serenity to accept the things I cannot change, courage to change the things I can, and wisdom to know the difference." We are not as familiar with the longer ending:

> Living one day at a time;
> Enjoying one moment at a time;

---

13. Jürgen Moltmann, *Theology of Hope: On the Ground and the Implications of a Christian Eschatology* (Minneapolis: Fortress Press, 1993), 32.

Accepting hardship as the pathway to peace;
Taking, as He did, this sinful world
As it is, not as I would have it;
Trusting that He will make all things right
If I surrender to His will;
So that I may be reasonably happy in this life
And supremely happy with Him
Forever and ever in the next.
Amen.[14]

"Now" hope leads to *reasonable* happiness. "Then" hope leads to *supreme* happiness. We need them both. Christ taught us to pray, "your kingdom come, your will be done, on earth as it is in heaven" (Matt 6:10, NIV). We need to seek God for the inbreaking of God's kingdom *now*. Nicholas Wolterstorff said, "I hold that it is a theological mistake . . . to see hope for consummation as the only legitimate form of Christian hope."[15] There's hope that things can change in this world by God's grace, the hope that sin and shame don't have the last word. There is a redeemer.

In difficult times, large sectors of humanity lean toward a raw Stoicism. Christians are prone to this temptation as much as others. Listen again to the wise old Quaker:

> The Stoic of any generation need not deny the existence of God; what he rejects is the Christian insistence that, in communion with God, prayer can make or should make an objective difference. There is no doubt that many of us, if we examine our positions fearlessly, will find that we are closer to Epictetus than we are to Christ. We tend to place more emphasis, in our prayers, upon acceptance of "that which cannot be changed" than upon the importunity of the widow who sought to change "that which can be changed."[16]

A "now" hope is a Christlike attitude. By God's grace things can change for the good.

---

14. Reinhold Niebuhr, "Serenity Prayer," available online at https://www.soberspeak.com/post/the-long-version-of-the-serenity-prayer.

15. Nicholas Wolterstorff, "Seeking Justice in Hope," in *The Future of Hope: Christian Tradition amid Modernity and Postmodernity*, ed. Miroslav Volf and William Katerberg (Grand Rapids, MI: Eerdmans, 2004), 82.

16. Trueblood, *A Place to Stand*, 87.

We adopt the attitude of hope by viewing all of life with the eyes of ultimate hope. God is the one who raised Jesus from the grave, the same one who delivered Israel from Egypt. Hope is a two-winged raven. It feeds us the bread of survival and life. Robert Jensen wrote, "We do not have the luxury of despair right now. There is too much at stake for too many people."[17] Hope is an attitude we adopt for ourselves that brings good to others.

## When Warnings Flash and Mountains Quake

Positive attitudes, sanctified self-talk, and self-encouragement in the Lord can carry us, and the communities that we serve, a long way toward reasonable happiness. These strategies can raise our attitudinal "grade" from a C- to a B or lift a B to an A+. Incremental adjustments are tremendously valuable; ask any of the countless students who have remained in school by raising their first-semester GPA from a 2.2 to a 3.2 in the spring. Simple strategies have a transformative impact on individuals and entire congregations.

But what happens when the starting point is not a C- but a failing grade? If Jensen is right that there's too much at stake to despair, where do we turn when despair settles over us anyway?

Have you ever seen a warning light flash on your dashboard? We've all seen the check engine light illuminate, and most of us have ignored it for far too long. Mine has been shining for four months and counting. But have you seen one *flash*? Several years ago during a family road trip, the check engine light began to strobe on a remote stretch of east Texas highway. After a quick web search about what the warning might mean, my wife said, "Pull over *right now*." If we had ignored this flashing beacon, the entire engine could have burned up. We had a real problem, and we needed help beyond ourselves.

Warnings flare from time to time in our spiritual lives too. When our attitudes bottom out, we need more than encouraging words from the person in the mirror or the Serenity Prayer to persevere. No one is immune from these crises. One of the most notable examples from the Scriptures is the story of Elijah. Just a chapter after the Lord nourishes him from the beaks of DoorDash ravens (1 Kings 17:1-7), Elijah defies and defeats the

---

17. Robert Jensen, "Why I Will Not Rally Around the President," *Counterpunch*, September 15, 2001, https://www.counterpunch.org/2001/09/15/why-i-will-not-rally-around-the-president/.

assembled prophets of Baal (1 Kings 18). He declares, "I, even I only, am left a prophet of the LORD," yet God vindicates him against 450 adversaries and the wicked King Ahab (1 Kings 18:22, NRSV).[18]

Rather than basking in victory, however, Elijah succumbs to despair. When Queen Jezebel threatens to execute him, he "was terrified . . . got up and ran for his life" (1 Kings 19:3). As he reaches the desert, he collapses beneath a scrub bush, where he "longed for his own death: 'It's more than enough, LORD! Take my life . . .'" (19:4). He took his death for granted but preferred to go at the Lord's hand rather than Jezebel's. He finally falls asleep and awakes to a surprise: an angel rouses him with fresh-baked bread and water. After a second sleep, Elijah awakes to another angelic breakfast before embarking on a forty-day journey to "Horeb, God's mountain" (19:8). Elijah is still fleeing, but now he has a better destination than a deserted broom tree. He runs to where he hopes the Lord can be found.

When Elijah reaches Horeb, the Lord does meet him and asks a simple question: "Why are you here, Elijah?" (1 Kings 19:9). A succession of signs and wonders ensues. All the hallmarks of epiphany parade before Elijah, all the ways that God has spoken in the past: hurricane wind, stone-shattering earthquake, blazing fire. After each one comes the same surprising refrain: "The LORD wasn't there." And then, in the stillness, "there was a sound. Thin. Quiet" (19:12). Have you ever heard a *thin* sound? Elijah recognizes that something is different; he draws closer but veils his face as he does. The voice comes again and asks the same question as before: "Why are you here, Elijah?" (19:13).

The prophet answers as before, but this time the Lord has specific instructions. He tells Elijah to anoint a new king of Aram and a new king of Israel—King Ahab will not endure! Perhaps most importantly, the Lord tells Elijah "anoint Elisha from Abel-meholah, Shaphat's son, to succeed you as prophet" (19:16). God promises the lonely prophet a protégé and a friend. And Elisha is not the only one! The Lord assures Elijah that he is far from alone. Seven thousand remain faithful to the God of Abraham, Isaac, and Jacob against the temptations of Baal.

What does this wild and wonderful story teach us about attitude, especially in the face of despair? First, no one is above despair. Elijah

---

18. Scripture quotations marked "NRSV" are from the New Revised Standard Version of the Bible, copyright 1989, by the Division of Christian Education of the National Council of the Churches of Christ in the U.S.A., and are used by permission. All rights reserved.

plummeted after one of the signal victories in all of Scripture. These triumphant moments are often when we are paradoxically at our most vulnerable, crippled by expectations (whether actual or merely projected) to sustain success. We often encourage our own church staff with the words of Heisman-winning philosopher Cam Newton: "When God be blessin', the Devil be messin.'"[19] Second, a genuine crisis of attitude impacts our whole being and demands an equally holistic response. Elijah's discouragement crippled his body, and God addressed these practical needs before even attempting to speak to the hurting prophet. Sound sleep and simple meals can work wonders. Notice that someone else met these needs for Elijah. Don't resist the helpers that God graciously provides, whether they arrive as doctors, counselors, or simple casserole-bearers. Third, Elijah positions himself to hear from the Lord. He runs, but he runs to the mountain where he expects God to appear. Sometimes we urgently need to change our surroundings, but "when you run, make sure you run *to something* and not away from."[20] There he discovers anew that our good God cares. God sees and hears, speaks and heals. God also returns us to community to carry on the work to which we are called. After a renewing retreat, God returns Elijah to fellowship among friends.

## Conclusion

As we think together about the constituent parts that make up our congregation's or Christian organization's soul culture, let's return to our mixing bowl metaphor. If we are working a batch of organizational dough, beliefs are the flour. Beliefs are bottom and basic. No flour, no bread. We submit that attitude is the yeast, the leavening agent, the activator. If our beliefs are solid but our attitudes are off, the bread will be flat or funky. As you analyze your congregation's or organization's soul culture, give careful attention to attitude. What does it feel like? Is it an environment where people are manifesting joy, gratitude, humility, and hope? What needs to be done to cultivate these attitudes in your soul and in the soul culture? What mood are you making?

---

19. Quoted in Andy Hutchins, "Cam Newton on NCAA Investigation: 'When God Be Blessin', the Devil Be Messin'," *SB Nation*, November 6, 2010, https://www.sbnation.com/ncaa-football/2010/11/6/1798163/cam-newton-ncaa-investigation-quote.

20. The Avett Brothers, "The Weight of Lies," by Seth Avett and Scott Avett, track 4 on *Emotionalism*, 2007.

Chapter 3

# Attitudes

## Questions for Further Reflection

1. "Jesus was funny" are the first words of this chapter. Are you accustomed to thinking of Jesus this way? Why (not)?

2. Read through a section of the Gospels, maybe even the entire Gospel of Mark. Jot some notes of where you see Jesus working the dough of his disciples' attitudes, with humor or otherwise:

3. How has your attitude been lately? If you were going to assign a letter grade, what would it be? Think about various aspects of your life and places where you are involved. What has your attitude been towards these places and the people you're around there? Is there any place that you think you could use an "attitude adjustment"?

Spend a few minutes in prayer about what you've written.

4. How do you respond to Charles Swindoll's claim, "[Life] is 10% what happens to me, and 90% how I react to it"?

5. Read Philippians 2:5-11 again. As a matter of fact, go ahead and read the entire letter. It will probably take less than fifteen minutes. In it the apostle Paul highlights four characteristics of a Christlike attitude:

(1) Joy
(2) Gratitude
(3) Humility
(4) Hope

How do these four relate to one another? Circle the one that comes most readily to you. Now underline the one that's the greatest challenge. Spend a few more minutes in prayer. Thank God for where you see a Christlike attitude within yourself, and ask for help in the areas where you struggle.

6. Read 1 Kings 18–19. Have you ever experienced the sort of highs and lows that Elijah encounters here? Has the "warning light" of your attitude ever begun to flash? What did you do next?

The Lord responds to Elijah's despair with compassion and practical help. God provides

(1) Rest
(2) Good, simple food and drink
(3) Word from God
(4) The fellowship of community

Each of us needs all four of these gifts to run the race set before us, especially when our personal warning lights begin to glow and eventually flash. Circle the one that you need most today. What practical steps can you take to receive it today?

# Chapter 3: Attitudes

## *Group Discussion Guide*

1. How does the overall attitude of our church or ministry "feel"? If you had to describe it using only one adjective, which one would you choose? *(Record responses on a whiteboard or flip chart.)* Is there any aspect of our fellowship that needs an attitude adjustment?

2. When has the attitude of others around you—whether at work, church, school, etc.—impacted your own attitude? Can you give an example (without naming names!), whether positive or negative? *(This prompt may work best in smaller table groups or pairs.)*

3. Read 1 Samuel 30:6 aloud together:

"David was in deep trouble because the troops were talking about stoning him. Each of the soldiers was deeply distressed about their sons and daughters. But David found strength in the LORD his God."

What does it mean to encourage ourselves in God as David did? Are there certain biblical passages or stories that help you find encouragement? How have you experienced God's word adjusting your attitude and encouraging you? *(List examples together—you'll likely want to save these responses for later.)*

4. Coach Grant Teaff encourages Christians to begin each day by setting their personal attitudes. How can we intentionally adopt the right attitude each day? Are there practical steps to take or even simple reminders that can help as we get ready in the morning?

5. Attitude is powerful. Both a positive and a negative attitude seem to be contagious. Can you think of someone who seems to suck the life out of a room or one who seems to fill it with laughing gas? What about these people's attitudes seems to create this kind of effect? Share an example of a person who makes a room feel lighter when they walk into it. *(Consider discussing this question in small groups and then returning to share a few examples with everyone.)*

6. How does our church manifest joy, gratitude, humility, and hope?

| | |
|---|---|
| **Joy** | |
| **Gratitude** | |
| **Humility** | |
| **Hope** | |

Which one of these attitudes is strongest among our congregation? Circle it. Are there any attitudes where we find ourselves lacking?

7. Dietrich Bonhoeffer described the people of Harlem's Abyssinian Baptist Church as full of "reserved melancholy and eruptive joy." What do you think he meant? How does his description connect with Jesus as both "a man of sorrows" and "a man of joy"?

8. Baylor's basketball coach Scott Drew fosters a culture of joy among his teams by emphasizing Jesus, others, and you in descending priority:

| |
|---|
| **Jesus** |
| **Others** |
| **You** |

How does it look to give priority to these things *in this order* in your life?

9. Divide into small groups and read the following texts. What does each one teach about the attitudes of joy and gratitude?

- Nehemiah 8:10
- Hebrews 12:1-2

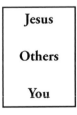

- Philippians 4:4-6
- Philippians 2:1-11

10. Christlike hope requires us to view the world as a two-tiered reality, with reasonable hope for the present world and supreme hope for the life to come. What are some examples of “now hope” and “then hope”? What are the sources of your hope?

11. I (Josh) end every night with my toddler daughter by asking her, “What do you want to thank God for?” She has some interesting responses! What do *you* want to thank God for? *(List responses, and then spend some significant time in prayer thanking God for God’s good gifts to your community.)*

# 4. Values

> *"Stop collecting treasures for your own benefit on earth, where moth and rust eat them and where thieves break in and steal them. Instead, collect treasures for yourselves in heaven, where moth and rust don't steal them. Where your treasure is, there your heart will be also."*
>
> Matthew 6:19-21

X marks the spot! Treasure! We've all wanted some of Chester Copperpot's rich stuff. Most of us had a pirate dream or two in our early childhood. In our minds we ran with young Jim Hawkins and the Goonies. By the time we entered the teenage years, the treasure we sought normally shifted from Spanish doubloons to a set of wheels and plenty of gasoline. My (Matt's) vehicular dream materialized in the form of a rust-colored (and rust-spotted) Jeep CJ-7.

The CJ was a cool ride. It was slightly lifted with a soft top. My friends and I rode freely around town and on the country roads outside of Meridian, Mississippi. We rolled about enjoying life in motion. We might have also been looking for more treasure. When you have a little, you seem to want more. The roll slowed one fine day, and I learned an early lesson about moths, rust, and thieves and about how slippery treasure can be.

The plan was to meet a friend at Lonnie and Pat's Café. We were going to eat the best burger in town. At least, that was what some claimed. The folks at New's Restaurant, Dexter's Café, and dozens of others would fight you over this claim, but truth be told, the Lonnie and Pat's burger was fine. It was a sunny day, and all was right with the world.

Lonnie and Pat's sat atop a big, kudzu-covered hill. I parked in a rush because my mind had wandered to onion rings. In my hurry, I failed to park the Jeep successfully. Parking is basic to driving, and I completely blew it. When I put my hand on Lonnie and Pat's doorknob, a woman running out of the café met me, shouting, "There's a baby in that Jeep!" From her seat inside, she had seen my tackle box fly out and get swallowed by the kudzu. She mistook it for a little human. I assured her that it was just a box of lures, and she went back relieved to her gigantic melamine coffee mug and Marlboro 100. Only then did I realize, much to my own chagrin, that the tackle box that wasn't a baby had flown out of a Jeep CJ-7 that the kudzu had also swallowed whole. Japan's little joke on the American South does control erosion, but it can also consume your treasure.

To extract and repair that Jeep would require a small chest of pirate's booty. The solution came in the form of a garage sale. Technically it was more like a carport sale. Family and friends rummaged through dust-covered stacks of stuff and gave offerings to the cause. On a dreary Saturday morning, folks showed up to haggle over our possessions. Things we had once wanted and spent money to purchase. Former gifts we had received with gratitude. Some of it got broken. Some of it was stolen. Piece by piece the crowd took our lusterless treasures. We eventually called it a day, glad it was over.

We eked out enough to resurrect the Jeep, but in the wise words of Burl Cain, "Nothing stays fixed." That Jeep rolled on for a few more years but is now only a memory. So is Lonnie and Pat's. If you search for the café on the internet, you will likely find its last Yelp review. The review reads, "Wanted a burger—planned stop on road trip—totally bummed." The review includes the photograph of a hand-scribbled sign on the door that reads, "Due to lack of business May 8th will be our last day to be open. Thank you for your business. Lonnie and Pat's Café."

John Prine captured this feeling of loss in his song "Souvenirs." He sang of his hatred for old pawn shops: "For they always bring me tears. I can't forgive the way they robbed me of my childhood souvenirs."[1] Moths. Rust. Thieves. They all have their way. This hard lesson is why we must embrace the values of Christ.

Values are one's judgments about what is important in life. Cultures have values. A culture's values are its ideas about what is good, right, fair, and just. Like individuals, a culture evaluates by judging what is important. People and cultures pursue, measure, reward, promote, and celebrate according to their values. Values are a vital part of your soul's vitality and the health of congregational soul culture.

Far too much current conversation about values, even within the church, adopts the basic assumptions and even the jargon of the business world. In chapter 1 we noted how even the term "values" often triggers us to

---

1. John Prine, "Souvenirs," track 3 on *Diamonds in the Rough*, 1972.

tune out in anticipation of yet another "corporate word salad." The British Broadcasting Corporation sent up this idea in a tremendous example of self-parody a few years ago. In their comedy series *W1A*, Hugh Bonneville plays an executive hired by the BBC as their new "Head of Values." When confronted early in his tenure about "some of the advantages of cutting his current salary," he naturally protests: "If ever there was an opportunity for the BBC to stand tall and make a big, bold statement about how much it values . . . the idea of valuing values, surely this is it. . . . I just don't see how the Head of Values cutting his own salary in half does that."[2] His comments provide sharp satire on the circular rationale of "valuing values." They also reveal that far too often, discussions of value are thinly dressed marketing ploys.

Jesus offers a far different way. The Sermon on the Mount is Jesus's message on kingdom values. Matthew 6:19-33 records how Jesus used economic terms to address the things he believed were most important in life. He wanted his people to understand and embrace what has *ultimate* value. In this great text, Jesus issued both a warning and an invitation.

The Lord warned us against placing ultimate value in things that careen downhill, close for lack of business, rust, mildew, and get stolen. He said, "Stop collecting treasures for your own benefit on earth" (Matt 6:19). Things on earth are fragile. Moths and rats gobble up earthly treasures, and thieves often lurk in the shadows. A disenchanted world offers little hope that we can pursue realities that have lasting value. In the face of this hopeless prospect, Jesus offers an invitation.

He implies an invitation to his better way in the question found in Matthew 6:25: "Isn't life more than food and the body more than clothes?" Food and clothes are basic to life. We must have them. They energize and protect our bodies, and without them we die. These needs are common to all humanity. Jesus said, "Gentiles long for all these things. Your heavenly Father knows that you need them" (6:32). They are important realities. If the materialists are correct, then they are really *all* we need. We simply need food, clothes, and shelter, and everything is permissible in pursuit of these needs. We can laser-focus on the self because this life is it. If the materialists are right, then earthly treasure is all there is to value. Jesus says they are wrong. In doing so, he places a huge question mark over the modern

---

2. *W1A*, season 1, episode 3, written and directed by John Morton, aired April 2, 2014, on BBC Two; clip available at https://www.youtube.com/watch?app=desktop&v=U5R4oKwPm5A.

notion of a closed universe. His invitation is to more life than materialists can fathom.

Jesus's warning and invitation correspond to two completely different sources of values. The first source originates in the self. The second source originates in God. In this chapter we will label these different value clusters as secreted and synchronized values.

## Secreted Values

French philosopher Jean-Paul Sartre gave the description "secreted" to self-generated, earthbound values. Sartre was a committed atheist firmly dedicated to the notion that existence precedes essence. This idea is a central claim of his philosophy, known as existentialism. Humans have no ultimate purpose. We have no given, elevated values to pursue. What we do have is choice and responsibility. Sartre believed all talk of values is wicked if we do not begin with the sober admission that we make them up as we go. He wrote, "Man secretes his own nothingness."[3] From Sartre's perspective, "[Values], like nothingness, enter the world only through human beings, through us, and we live like dirty pigs if we do not acknowledge that we have introduced them and bear the responsibility for acting on them."[4]

Self-generated values come out of us like sweat and tears. We are their origin. So much of life is given to their pursuit that we confuse this quest with life itself. Quite often this pursuit proves so disappointingly trivial. This realization was Paul's experience when the Way, Truth, and Life in the form of the glorified Jesus confronted him. His conversion led to a reevaluation of his values.

We learn about Paul's experience in Philippians 3. He outlined his pedigree and achievements. Paul was a shining star by every measure of his culture. He had the social, physical, educational, religious, and economic advantages required to take off like a rocket in life. He was zealous and hard working. Paul simply trucked his peers. He said, "If anyone else has reason to put their confidence in physical advantages, I have even more" (Phil 3:4). Then he met Christ.

When Paul shared his life story, he opened his cumulative portfolio for all to see and said, "These things were my assets, but I wrote them off as a loss for the sake of Christ. But even beyond that, I consider everything

---

3. Jean-Paul Sartre, *Being and Nothingness*, quoted in T. Z. Lavine, *From Socrates to Sartre: The Philosophic Quest* (New York: Bantam, 1984), 356.

4. Lavine, *From Socrates to Sartre*, 369.

a loss in comparison with the superior value of knowing Christ Jesus my Lord. I have lost everything for him, but what I lost I think of as sewer trash, so that I might gain Christ and be found in him" (Phil 3:7-9a). After turning to Christ, Paul reappraised his treasure. He discovered there was indeed more than earthly achievement and acclaim. That which was once valuable to him he discounted as waste. Mere human values lost their luster in the light of the risen Lord.

The book of Ecclesiastes also offers an appraisal of secreted values. It chronicles hot pursuits under the sun. The Teacher of Ecclesiastes narrated his adventures chasing all the world has to offer. He applied his mind to learning, his body to pleasure, his cunning to power, and his effort to riches. He was successful in each attempt. The Teacher drank life to the dregs. If anyone was worthy of the redundant phrase "lived experience," it was the Teacher of the Assembly. He declared all of life under the sun "pointless." There is an odd angle in Ecclesiastes. The Teacher was able to see and live pointless pursuits without growing bitter or despondent. Why? Peter J. Leithart observes, "So Solomon sees all this without falling into Foucault's Nietzchean despair and pessimism. . . . Solomon's unblinking examination of power and oppression is pervaded by an eschatological faith that this world of tears under the sun is not the only world, a confidence that there is a time after the time under the sun."[5] This perspective led to the stunning conclusion of the Teacher's work: "So this is the end of the matter; all has been heard. Worship God . . ." (Eccl 12:13).

The Teacher's message to honor God in a world that can seem pointless and Paul's testimony about the relative values of earthly treasure are biblical examples of leaders shaping soul culture. Paul spoke to the church and Solomon addressed Israel, but both were working on the collective culture of the Lord's assembly. This social situation is important to note because all values are in large measure socially conditioned. Cultural forces press secreted values out of us. Several thinkers help us put our minds around this idea.

Charles Taylor calls these shaping forces "the social imaginary." Listen to how he describes it:

> I want to speak of "social imaginary" here, rather than social theory, because there are important differences between the two. There are, in

---

5. Peter J. Leithart, *Solomon among the Postmoderns* (Grand Rapids, MI: Brazos Press, 2008), 163.

> fact, several differences. I speak of "imaginary" (i) because I'm talking about the way ordinary people "imagine" their social surroundings, and this is often not expressed in theoretical terms, it is carried in images, stories, legends, etc. But it is also the case that (ii) theory is often the possession of a small minority, whereas what is interesting in the social imaginary is that it is shared by large groups of people, if not the whole society. Which leads to a third difference: (iii) the social imaginary is that common understanding which makes possible common practices, and a widely shared sense of legitimacy.[6]

Our social imaginary gives us an intuitive sense of the way things should be. The values we think come from us really emerge from a larger cultural imagination. External pressures push out the sweat and tears.

Peter Berger's idea of plausibility structures illustrates why some values seem almost self-evident while others are repugnant.[7] Michel Foucault uses the term *dispositif* or dispositive to refer to the various institutional, physical, and administrative mechanisms and knowledge structures that enhance and maintain the exercise of power within the social body. All this scaffolding works together to create what *feels* like choice and responsibility, when really it is conforming to the hive mind. Secreted values that seem so individualistic really secrete from fallen societies. The general public lives downstream from the elite notions and institutions that wrangle power in the world. We can be so bold as to call these influences and influencers principalities. This helps explain the truth of Catholic Bishop Robert Barron's statement, "What was once whispered in the cafes of Paris is now the default position of the American teenager."[8]

Paul understood these ideas years ago when he said, "Don't be conformed to the patterns of this world, but be transformed by the renewing of your minds so that you can figure out what God's will is—what is good and pleasing and mature" (Rom 12:2). As J. B. Phillips paraphrased it, "Don't let the world around you squeeze you into its own mold . . . ."[9] The pattern and mold of this world sounds a great deal like a dispositif or social

---

6. Charles Taylor, *A Secular Age* (Cambridge, MA: Belknap Press, 2007), 171–72.

7. See Peter Berger, *The Sacred Canopy: Elements of a Sociological Theory of Religion* (New York: Anchor, 1991).

8. Robert Barron, "Understanding the Present Moment #4: Michel Foucault," *Word on Fire Show*, 2022, available at https://www.youtube.com/watch?v=Py_4NBfCDnU&t=19s.

9. J. B. Phillips, *The New Testament in Modern English* (New York: MacMillan, 1958).

imaginary. The command in Romans 12:2 says that there is a vital alternative: the will of God. Values driven by the will of God are synchronized values.

## Synchronized Values

Ben Harper once sang, "Make sure that the fortune you seek is the fortune that you need."[10] The danger of chasing worldly values is that we just might get what we want. A. J. Conyers pointed out this danger:

> Hope longs for that which is not, and ceases to exist when what is hoped for is attained. It is the wellspring of work, imagination, moral responsibility. It is that which draws for us the connection between what is, what ought to be, and what might be. So the fastening of hope on temporal rewards theoretically threatens the extinction of hope because, the awful fact is, you might get what you hope for. And, then, with hope gone, only "amusement" is left.[11]

David Brooks called this awful fact "climbing the first mountain."[12] There is a more holy mountain and a more hopeful pursuit.

According to Jesus, the fortune we need is heavenly treasure. Pursuing this fortune requires a hopeful vision for a time after our time under the sun. It requires a settled faith in a transcendent God who is interested in human affairs. P. T. Forsyth's 1907 observation seems pertinent here: "If within us we find nothing over us we succumb to that which is around us."[13] Synchronized values wed the "over us" to the "within us," protecting us from the secreted values all "around us."

Synchronized means "arising at the same time." One of the most spellbinding Olympic events is synchronized swimming. Each of the participants moves in harmony with the others. The unity is inspiring. Our desire as followers of Jesus should be for our values to align with Christ's, to move in sync with him. A vivid biblical image helps us see that this alignment has

---

10. Ben Harper, "Diamonds on the Inside," track 3 on *Diamonds on the Inside*, 2003.

11. A. J. Conyers, *Eclipse of Heaven: The Loss of Transcendence and Its Effect on Modern Life* (South Bend, IN: St. Augustine's Press, 1999), 62.

12. David Brooks, *The Second Mountain: The Quest for a Moral Life* (New York: Random House, 2020), xvi.

13. P. T. Forsyth, *Peter Taylor Forsyth (1848–1921): Director of Souls*, ed. Harry Escott (London: Epworth Press, 1948).

been God's desire for people all along. The image is walking with God. We read in Amos 3:3, "Will two people walk together unless they have agreed to do so?" Before Amos, we had the mysterious example of Enoch. Twice in as many verses in Genesis, Scripture says that "Enoch walked with God" (Gen 5:22, 24). The image of walking with God helps us embrace the idea that we don't inhabit a closed universe. The transcendent God enters the field to abide with us.

For our souls to be well and for the soul cultures of our congregations to be healthy, we need to cultivate the awareness that God is near and is active in our lives. We should embrace what God embraces and shun what God shuns. When we walk with God, we don't walk as peers; instead, we walk as those being led by an experienced guide. This is God's world, after all, and God knows the way. Paul's word in Galatians is helpful at this point:

> I say be guided by the Spirit and you won't carry out your selfish desires. A person's selfish desires are set against the Spirit, and the Spirit is set against one's selfish desires. They are opposed to each other, so you shouldn't do whatever you want to do. But if you are being led by the Spirit you aren't under the Law. The actions that are produced by selfish motives are obvious, since they include sexual immorality, moral corruption, doing whatever feels good, idolatry, drug use and casting spells, hate, fighting, obsession, losing your temper, competitive opposition, conflict, selfishness, group rivalry, jealousy, drunkenness, partying, and other things like that. (Gal 5:16-21)

The vices that Paul lists read like a Twitter thread; these same things plague our world today. Many secular voices are calling for social justice. To put it bluntly, there is no justice absent a robust doctrine of sin and salvation. Nietzsche had the courage to recognize that the demise of God means everything is permitted[14]—you are free to do whatever you want to do. A commitment to synchronized values opposes this idea. It faithfully affirms that God is alive and humbly committed to walking with and leading us by the Spirit of Christ. Only then can genuine justice and mercy emerge and ultimately flourish. In the words of Micah 6:8, "And what does the LORD require of you? To act justly and to love mercy and to *walk humbly with your God*" (NIV, emphasis added).

---

14. See Friedrich Nietzsche, *Beyond Good and Evil: On the Genealogy of Morality*, trans. Adrian Del Caro (Stanford, CA: Stanford University Press, 2014).

My (Matt's) grandmother's name was Geraldine Fleming Heblon. Most folks called her Jerry, but I called her Gran. We lived near Gran when I was growing up. My brothers and I were able to spend a good bit of time with her, and time with Gran was always interesting.

Many of my favorite memories are of Gran at the piano. She played by ear and played for fun. She could transition from Fannie Crosby hymns to hot boogie-woogie in a Memphis minute. She often brought me in on the act. ("Act" is hardly the right word since the audience was nearly nonexistent. Gran didn't even have a cat.)

Gran bought me a ukulele on a Saturday shopping trip to the Peavey's Melody Music Store. I still remember picking it out and the old salesman playing "Ghost Riders in the Sky." He reminded me that Jimmie Rodgers played the ukulele. I now wonder why he didn't play one of the Blue Yodeler's Hawaiian classics. I guess it skipped his mind; life is full of lost opportunities. I never learned to play the ukulele properly, but when I faked it, I felt like Elvis.

Gran would bang on the piano, and I would fake-play the ukulele. We could do our routine for hours. One day she said, "Matt, would you like to write a song?" I could fake-play a ukulele, so why not fake some songwriting? I said, "Sure."

Gran played a while and then got out her steno pad and felt-tip pen. She scribbled down these lines:

> I know a secret too good to be true.
> If you will let me, I'll share it with you.
> Rainbows and moonbeams will carry us through.
> That is the secret I'm sharing with you.

I think I knew even then that this wasn't great poetry. I've memorized and forgotten hundreds of lines of truly great poetry at this point in my life, but I've never forgotten those words from Gran. I still sing them today.

What is a rainbow? It's a sign of God's promise. What is a moonbeam? A moonbeam is reflected light. The light comes from the sun. Gran's little song contains the raw material for not just a secret but a revelation. As followers of Christ, God's covenant promises (the word) carry us, and we reflect the light of the Son (the Word). Synchronized values happen when the word and the Spirit of Christ light our lives and we in turn reflect that light in the world.

## Synchronicity and the Sermon on the Mount

Let's agree at this point that we are going to reject selfish secreted values and instead go after values that align with Christ. How do we do it? Is there a key? We suggest that Jesus lays out key elements in Matthew 6. Three words will help us wrap our minds around the concepts. The words are presence, peace, and provision.

### *Presence*

Jesus gave us a powerful image in the Sermon on the Mount. Perhaps you will remember it from your Sunday school felt board lessons. We even sang about it back in the day: "This little light of mine. I'm going to let it shine." The indwelling Christ is the key to living out synchronized values. Jesus said,

> The eye is the lamp of the body. Therefore, if your eye is healthy, your whole body will be full of light. But if your eye is bad, your whole body will be full of darkness. If then the light in you is darkness, how terrible that darkness will be! No one can serve two masters. Either you will hate the one and love the other, or you will be loyal to the one and have contempt for the other. You cannot serve God and wealth. (Matt 6:22-24)

We must choose a ground and object of ultimate value. It's either God or "stuff." It can't be both, and our eyes tell the tale. Another way of rendering "good eye" is "single eye." David Garland describes the function of the single eye this way: "A single eye shines forth the presence of inner light. . . . It is bad enough to be in the dark but worse to have the darkness in you. Being generous with one's possessions is a sign that one has moved into the world of light."[15] Christ can dwell in our hearts by faith. In his absence the world will reign over our interior lives. Bob Dylan captured this in his song "False Prophet": "I know how it happened, I saw it begin. I opened my heart to the world and the world came in."[16] Mammon is the world. It is more than mere money. It is the false promise that we can live securely without God. It's every idol. The indwelling Christ expels this darkness from our souls and from our soul cultures. If we want to

---

15. David E. Garland, *Reading Matthew: A Literary and Theological Commentary* (Macon, GA: Smyth & Helwys Publishing, 2013), 81.

16. Bob Dylan, "False Prophet," track 2 of *Rough and Rowdy Ways*, 2020.

synchronize our values with God's, we won't do it by gritty effort alone. We need what Thomas Chalmers called "the expulsive power of a new affection."[17]

## Peace

Some of Jesus's most memorable words are in Matthew 6:25-34:

> Therefore, I say to you, don't worry about your life, what you'll eat or what you'll drink, or about your body, what you'll wear. Isn't life more than food and the body more than clothes? Look at the birds in the sky. They don't sow seed or harvest grain or gather crops into barns. Yet your heavenly Father feeds them. Aren't you worth much more than they are? Who among you by worrying can add a single moment to your life? And why do you worry about clothes? Notice how the lilies in the field grow. They don't wear themselves out with work, and they don't spin cloth. But I say to you that even Solomon in all of his splendor wasn't dressed like one of these. If God dresses grass in the field so beautifully, even though it's alive today and tomorrow it's thrown into the furnace, won't God do much more for you, you people of weak faith? Therefore, don't worry . . . .

Did you catch the value judgment Jesus made here? He said, "You are worth more than birds." He made a straightforward evaluation. Peter Singer's evaluation would be that Jesus was being a great sinner here. The sin? Speciesism. Singer and Jesus can't both be right. In the words of Elton Trueblood, "Unless the law of noncontradiction is regarded as the necessary condition of all rational discussion, we give up everything."[18]

Jesus gets to evaluate. That's the Christian position. He says human worth is the concern of God and that we can therefore live lives of faith and trust. No, this certainly does not mean that nothing bad will ever befall us. It does mean that we will ultimately be well and that our days will be full of life. We can live at peace in the world because Christ has given us his peace. This way of life is unique. It contrasts grasping with receiving, surviving with living. C. S. Lewis captured this beautifully when he said, "Friendship is unnecessary, like philosophy, like art, like the universe itself (for God did not need to create). It has no survival value; rather it is one of

---

17. Thomas Chalmers, *The Expulsive Power of a New Affection* (Wheaton, IL: Crossway, 2020).

18. David Elton Trueblood, *Philosophy of Religion* (New York: Harper and Brothers, 1957), 32.

those things which give value to survival."[19] Synchronized values give value to survival and hope for time after our time under the sun. Synchronized values include both the now and the later, the immanent and the transcendent. James Cone said it this way: "And so the transcendent and the immanent, heaven and earth, must be held together in critical, dialectical tension, each one correcting the limits of the other."[20]

Synchronized values, God's values concretized in the human person, animate just and compassionate action in the world and strengthen God's people to face the worst imaginable evils in this world. Cone points to a lynching testimony from 1899 to illustrate this awe-inspiring truth: "Before he was lynched in Oxford, Mississippi (1899), Steve Allen testified to his 'peace with God,' saying that 'Jesus died on the Roman cross for me; through his mercy all my sins are forgiven. I am anchored in Christ.' With that testimony, 'he went to his death without a tremor.'"[21] The light of Christ leads to peace "not as the world gives" (John 14:27).

## *Provision*

Jesus calls us to live by God's kind provision. Faith helps us clarify our values. It keeps us from confusing means and ends. Jesus reminds us that the Father knows we have needs and is committed to supplying them. Many congregations live by a myth of scarcity.[22] They forget the axiom of Hudson Taylor: "God's work, done God's way, will never lack God's supply."[23] When we lack faith, our values get warped, and we anxiously begin to grasp and claw.

---

19. C. S. Lewis, *The Four Loves* (San Diego, CA: Harcourt Brace Jovanovich, 1960), 103.

20. James H. Cone, *The Cross and the Lynching Tree* (Maryknoll, NY: Orbis, 2011), 156.

21. Ibid., 26.

22. See Andrew Root, *Churches and the Crisis of Decline: A Hopeful, Practical Ecclesiology for a Secular Age* (Grand Rapids, MI: Baker Academic, 2022).

23. Quoted by Leslie T. Lyall, *A Passion for the Impossible: The Continuing Story of the Mission Hudson Taylor Began* (London: OMF Books, 1965), 37.

## Possible Challenges for Soul Cultures that Embrace Synchronized Values

Let's assume we serve in a congregation that has heard Jesus say, "Instead, desire first and foremost God's kingdom and God's righteousness, and all these things will be given to you as well" (Matt 6:33). We want to live by faith and have our values align with Christ's. What are some of the challenges? We see at least three.

### *Challenge 1: The Danger of (Deliberately) Distorted Values*

We first need to be aware that there are those who intentionally twist Scripture and the way of Christ to take advantage of God's people. Wolves in sheep's clothes still ride around looking for a meal. Healthy Christian doctrine is a safeguard against them. This challenge has confronted soul cultures since Jude and 2 Peter and will be with us until the end.

### *Challenge 2: The Danger of Disordered Values*

The history of the church demonstrates far too readily the danger of misplaced values. When our values become disordered, they threaten to overpower beliefs and attitudes and poison the dough of our soul culture. Once this happens, our goals and practices grow corrupted to disastrous and even deadly consequences. Nowhere is this danger more evident than among the German churches of a century ago. In the aftermath of World War I, Germans revived nineteenth-century ideals of national unity and heroic leadership—worthy enough values in their own right. These hopes turned cancerous, however, as they fused with religious ideas and achieved ultimate significance. Nationalism replaced national pride, the *Führer* became a political messiah, and the swastika shrouded the altar of the Lord Jesus Christ as "the symbol of German hope."[24] Against this onslaught, Dietrich Bonhoeffer and fellow pastors within the Confessing Church insisted on the supremacy of Christ over all earthly counterfeits at tremendous personal cost.

We are no strangers to the danger of disordered values within our own country and kin. Our forebears in the Bible Belt have battled, and at times

24. Steve M. Bezner, "Understanding the World Better than It Understands Itself: The Theological Hermeneutics of Dietrich Bonhoeffer" (PhD dissertation, Baylor University, 2008), 98–100.

embraced, their own demons both before and since the Third Reich. J. B. Gambrell, whose admonition to "work our dough . . . so to culture our people as to bring them to a New Testament way of thinking and feeling"[25] launched this project and provided its guiding metaphor, was vulnerable to the racist value structures of his nineteenth-century world. As a Baptist denominational leader in Georgia, Mississippi, and Texas, Gambrell was both a product of his native Southern culture and an agent of its perpetuation. What he received by nature he cultivated by nurture. "A New Testament way of thinking and feeling" did not sufficiently shape his value of Black people, whom Christ loved and gave himself up to save. Rather than embracing Black people as bearers of God's image and recipients of his reconciling love, Gambrell perpetuated racist ideology virulent even by the standards of his own day, much less of the twenty-first century or the gospel. The values of his culture eclipsed his beliefs and tainted the lump of dough.[26]

These issues are personal for us authors. One of us has the middle name Lee, just like his father before him. When asked about memorials to the Southern Confederacy, I sometimes respond wryly, "I am one." The other's father-in-law served as Senate page to Strom Thurmond during the 1960s. There he had a front-row perspective on how misplaced values corrupted beliefs and consequently goals and practices at the highest levels of American political life.

The church's failures, past and present, and their painful consequences for the most vulnerable emphasize the critical need for a gospel "way of thinking and feeling." We need to attend to the claims of the gospel on our beliefs, attitudes, values, goals, *and* practices. All five ingredients must blend harmoniously or the recipe will fail, the dough will fall flat, and the loaf will grow bitter rather than life-giving. In the waning pages of the tremendously popular *Jesus and John Wayne*, Kristin Kobes Du Mez argues, "evangelicalism must be seen as a cultural and political movement rather than as a community defined chiefly by its theology."[27] Notice how

25. J. B. Gambrell, "Working a Batch of Dough," in *Parable and Precept* (New York: Revell, 1917), 63.

26. For more on Gambrell and on Lost Cause Southern religious culture more generally, see Charles Reagan Wilson, *Baptized in Blood: The Religion of the Lost Cause, 1865–1920*, rev. ed. (Athens, GA: University of Georgia Press, 2009).

27. Kristin Kobes Du Mez, *Jesus and John Wayne: How White Evangelicals Corrupted a Faith and Fractured a Nation* (New York: Liveright Publishing, 2020), 298.

she prioritizes culture *over* theology as the defining feature of evangelical life. Just a paragraph later, though, Du Mez nuances this view: "Rather than seeing culture as pitted against theology, however, we should treat the interplay between the two as what ultimately defines evangelicalism."[28] This appraisal is better, but it still misses the mark. It pits culture against theology as though the two exist independently from one another. The truth is that every theology emerges within a culture, and every culture takes shape from its predominant theology. Beliefs are one ingredient—a critical one no doubt—in the mixing bowl of soul culture. When the recipe goes wrong, as Du Mez argues that it has, we must respond wisely. We can't afford to throw out the bread of culture and starve, and it's just as foolish to bake bread without flour as to make bricks without straw. We need good theology, and we also need values formed by them under the guidance of the Spirit of Christ. We must work the dough.

By God's grace the church perseveres just as Jesus promised it would (Matt 16:18). "God perfects what we do badly," as Barth put it. The tragic missteps of prior generations should sensitize us to the utter fallibility of our own. Thanks be to God, God's "grace is enough . . . because power is made perfect in weakness" (2 Cor 12:9). Our churches and their leaders continue to lead with a limp.[29] It is up to us whether we heed the Spirit's call and limp toward greater justice and faithfulness or away from it.

### *Challenge 3: The Danger of Domesticated Values*

The third challenge is the temptation to domesticate Jesus and ask him to serve as a mascot for our own ambitions. We can trick ourselves into believing that we are doing so in service to Christ's agenda. Andy Root brilliantly diagnoses this tendency in his book *The Church after Innovation*.[30] We commend this work to you as you shape the soul culture of your congregation. Mike Judge may have oddly anticipated Root by artfully exploring this theme in a 2003 episode of the cartoon *King of the Hill*.

Hank Hill is the chief protagonist of this series set in suburban Texas. He lives with his wife Peg, their son Bobby, and the family dog Lady Bird. The title of season 8, episode 2 is "Reborn to Be Wild." In this episode

---

28. Ibid.

29. See Dan B. Allender, *Leading with a Limp* (Colorado Springs, CO: WaterBrook Press, 2008).

30. Andrew Root, *The Church After Innovation: Questioning Our Obsession with Work, Creativity, and Entrepreneurship* (Grand Rapids, MI: Baker Academic, 2022).

Bobby loses interest in the church that has shaped his life and links up instead with trendy Pastor K. Pastor K could be vulgar for the Lord. He'd do anything to gather a crowd. Hank is rightfully concerned about Bobby's soul health and what Pastor K's "reborn to be wild" soul culture is shaping in him. The final scene of the episode is funny, memorable, and touching.

Hank finally has enough and says, "Let's go, Bobby."

Bobby replies, "You can give me the stink eye all you want, but it's not going to change anything."

"Fine."

"But when I'm eighteen," Bobby continues, "I'm going to do whatever I want for the Lord. Tattoos, piercings, the works."

"Well, I'll take that chance," replies Hank. "Come here, there's something I want to show you." Things begin to turn more serious as Hank takes a box down from the garage shelf. "Remember this?"

"My Bean Bag Buddy? Oh, man, I can't believe I collected those things. They're so lame."

"You didn't think so five years ago. And how about your virtual pet? You used to carry this thing everywhere. Then you got tired of it, forgot to feed it, and it died."

"I look like such a dork," Bobby admits as he gazes at an old photo.

"I know how you feel," Hank agrees. "I never thought that Members Only jacket would go out of style. But it did." He continues to offer humble wisdom to his son: "I know you think that stuff you're doing is cool, but in a few years you're gonna think it's lame. And I don't want the, uh, Lord to, you know, end up in this box."

"I got you, Dad," Bobby acknowledges. Message received. "Hey, what's this picture? Mom used to have blond hair?"

"Farah Fawcett was very popular back then," Hank explains, concluding the lesson.[31]

Our biggest challenge in this age of congregational decline is not lack of resources or need of innovation. It is lack of vitality. Vitality is kindled when we synchronize our values to God's. God has promised presence, and we can live in God's peace. When we desire the kingdom above all else, God faithfully provides. Innovation is then born through the creative Spirit of Jesus rather than generated by the fickle, fidgety *Zeitgeist*.

---

31. *King of the Hill*, season 8, episode 2, "Reborn to Be Wild," directed by Dominic Polcino, written by Tony Gama-Lobo and Rebecca May, aired November 9, 2003, on Fox.

Chapter 4

# Values

## Questions for Further Reflection

1. Read through the Sermon on the Mount (Matthew 5–7) in a single sitting. What does Jesus value? How about the disciples?

Now repeat this same exercise with one of the epistles. Highlight where you see the same values from the Gospel reemerging.

2. Jesus warns us against placing undue value in the things that can rust, be moth-ridden, or roll down a kudzu patch. When and why do you find yourself tempted to value these things more than you should? How do you combat this temptation?

3. In the Sermon on the Mount, Jesus tells his disciples, "Where your treasure is, there your heart will be also" (Matt 6:21). If you're feeling courageous, pull up your most recent bank or credit card statement. Where has your treasure been going? Pay particular attention to discretionary spending, and list the top few categories below. How do these decisions relate to your answer to the previous question? Are there any surprises?

| | Category (e.g., clothing, dining, entertainment, gifts, etc.) | Amount Spent |
|---|---|---|
| 1 | | |
| 2 | | |
| 3 | | |
| 4 | | |

4. Read Philippians 3:1-11. How has your relationship with Christ changed the priority of your values? Are there things that you value now that you didn't value before? Are there things that you once prized that don't hold value for you anymore?

5. Matthew 6:19-24 promises the presence, peace, and provision of God. Jot down a few thoughts about what each of these promises means to you and about how they guide and influence what you value.

(1) Presence:

(2) Peace:

(3) Provision:

# Chapter 4: Values

## *Group Discussion Guide*

We've all encountered corporate values campaigns that are thinly disguised marketing ploys. The British comedy *W1A* lampoons this fad as the BBC hires an executive "Head of Values," and no one—including him—seems to know what to do next. The short clip (less than 2 ½ minutes) "Advantages of Cutting Your Salary" (https://www.youtube.com/watch?v=U5R4oK-wPm5A) may spark some discussion about the state of values in the public imagination.

1. The solution to this farce isn't to eliminate values but instead to grind them in something solid. Here's where the ingredients of soul culture begin to interact. How do we integrate values with beliefs and attitudes as we work our batch of dough?

2. Everyone values something. Prioritizing values is a basic function of human nature. Divide into small groups and discuss what each of the following values most. After 5 to 10 minutes, reconvene, share your responses, and record them on a whiteboard or flip chart.

- The surrounding culture
- Yourself
- Our church/ministry
- Christ

3. Worship defines and declares what we value most. Proclaiming value is a good working definition of worship. Consider your church's most recent worship service. *(Group leaders may want to bring leftover bulletin copies or a video recording of the service to guide conversation.)*

- Based on this worship service, what does your church value?
- Would an outside observer attending your church for the first time recognize the same values that you do?

4. Does your church or ministry have a mission statement or vision statement? *(Leaders, asking the group this question can be an invaluable diagnostic check. If participants are unsure whether a statement exists—or can't articulate*

*one that does—that is significant. We recommend asking the question cold to gauge responses, but then have your statement available to display or hand out for the rest of this exercise.)*

- What does the statement communicate about what you value?
- Does it reflect the congregation's *true* priorities, or is it more aspirational? *(Note that aspirational statements aren't necessarily bad. Our next chapter/session is entirely focused on goals! But we need to be honest with ourselves and with those we serve about what sort of function our statements accomplish.)*
- What are the *specific* values of *this* congregation?
- Have they adapted or evolved during your time here? *(Use the whiteboard to capture responses. Pay particular attention to the longest-tenured and newest members. The former have seen the most change—and continuity!—over time, and the latter presumably chose to join you due to their perception of some of these specific values.)*
- Which values are common to *all* churches, and which ones are particular to our own circumstance and vocation?

5. Have you ever witnessed someone using Jesus as a mascot to further their own interests or agendas? *(This can happen from nefarious manipulation, but it can also arise more sincerely as we confuse our values with Christ's rather than allowing his to become our own.)* Have you ever used Jesus as a mascot yourself? How do we resist this tendency in our own lives and in the life of the church? *(Discussion in smaller groups or pairs may produce the most honest answers here. You can then invite a few examples for the whole group.)*

6. Churches that embrace synchronized values still face challenges on several fronts. Which one(s) below do you think pose the greatest danger for our place and time? How can we resist diluting the values of Christ?

- (Deliberately) Distorted Values (from "wolves in sheep's clothing")
- Disordered Values (like the nationalism of many German churches in the 1930s and 1940s or the racism of far too many American churches, past and present)
- Domesticated Values (Recall Hank Hill's warning to his son Bobby: "I don't want the Lord to end up in this box.")

7. Jesus commands us to "desire first and foremost God's kingdom and God's righteousness" (Matt 6:33). In the same chapter he invites us to pray, "Bring in your kingdom so that your will is done on earth as it's done in heaven" (6:10). Many of us pray these words weekly, even daily. What do they mean practically?

8. Our friend Steve Bezner pastors in Houston and has led his congregation to pray, "In Houston as it is in heaven." What would it look like for your church or ministry to pray, "In [our town] as it is in heaven"? How might the coming kingdom of Christ look in your own time and place? What would change?

# 5. Goals

> *God's kingdom isn't about eating food and drinking but about righteousness, peace, and joy in the Holy Spirit. Whoever serves Christ this way pleases God and gets human approval. So let's strive for the things that bring peace and the things that build each other up.*
>
> **Romans 14:17-19**

"What's the point?"

Type these three words into your favorite search engine. If your algorithm is remotely like ours, you will likely scroll through many proposed answers to life's great question. Within the search results will be a quiz to determine if you are depressed. Before long, advertisements for online therapy and psychotropic drugs will magically appear on your various screens. Just try it. We double-dog dare you! The great existential question "What's the point?" has been with us for ages. When we raise this question in the little Google rectangle, the great algorithm, the virtual panopticon, tips off the market that our numbed online scrolling might be morphing into a genuine search. Marketers will try not to let that happen.

Famous thinkers and ordinary folks alike stop to ponder the point of it all. Does a singular point even exist? In chapter 4 we explored the vital role that values play in our individual and congregational lives. Values and the search for the point are fused to one another. If we believe that life has a point, we will value that point and make it our life's goal. If we deny that life has a point, we are left to concoct both our values and our goals from scratch. Goals, like values, are either secreted or synchronized. They ooze out of the self with the help of the ambient culture, or they are synchronized with God. Aligning our goals with God is a crucial Christian concern. Embracing an absolute goal and living toward it is now countercultural.

Many people believe that life is pointless even though longing for the point seems nearly universal. The reason Sartre, Nietzsche, Camus, and Foucault approached values the way they did is because they rejected an ultimate goal. We live downstream from these thinkers, and our culture is drinking the water. In Pauline language, they have influenced the "patterns of this world" (Rom 12:2).

I recall my first direct introduction to this way of thinking. It was not in a philosophy class; it was on a rental from Blockbuster Video. In 1994 Ben Stiller directed the film *Reality Bites*. Helen Childress wrote the screenplay and set the story in Houston, Texas. It has become something of a Gen-X cult classic. Ethan Hawke plays a brooding slacker philosopher named Troy Dyer. Winona Ryder plays Troy's longtime friend and sometime love interest Lelaina Pierce. The dialogue between them provides the intellectual spine of the story.

Perhaps the most memorable conversation between Troy and Lelaina overlooks the Gulf of Mexico. It became known as the seashell scene, and scores of forty-somethings memorized it verbatim when they were in their late teens. The heart of it is Troy's one-minute monologue:

> My parents got divorced when I was five years old. And I saw my father about three times a year after that. And when he found out that he had cancer he decided to bring me here and he gives me this big pink seashell and he says to me, "Son, the answers are all inside of this." And I'm like, "What?" But then I realized that the shell was empty. There's no point to any of this. It's all just a lottery of meaningless tragedy and a series of near escapes. So, I take pleasure in the details, you know. A Quarter-Pounder with cheese. Those are good. The sky about ten minutes before it starts to rain. The moment when your laughter becomes a cackle. And I sit back, and I smoke my Camel straights. And I ride my own melt.[1]

If you're unfamiliar with the phrase "ride my own melt," the Urban Dictionary defines it this way: "to go one's own way, enjoying the pleasure of the here and now and ignoring what others think." This life goal would eventually prove unsatisfying for Troy, but it has been around since ancient times. It is a resilient temptation. One could argue that the philosopher/preacher of Ecclesiastes was examining all the ways human beings ride their own melts. He kicked the tires on most of the here-and-now pleasures—pleasures of luxury, power, knowledge, and achievement. He went his own way because the ways are legion. He found them all wanting as an ultimate goal. Recall his final conclusion: "So this is the end of the matter; all has been heard. Worship God..." (Eccl 12:13). If God is God, then life has

---

1. *Reality Bites*, directed by Ben Stiller, Universal, 1994.

a point. That is the point, and it gives all the details value and meaning. When we talk about being goal-oriented Christians and encourage mixing goals into congregational soul culture, we are recognizing that professing Christian faith entails embracing the point, the goal God gives.

When we lose a "God is God" theology and view the church as the Rotary Club with better music, we twist its goals. The transcendent dimension of faith must be present if the immanent is to have any vitality. Charles Taylor points out how much of the church in the nineteenth century lost a vision for the point, the goal, and became thin-blooded. It pursued moralism, and the church lost its heft without a "God is God" theology. He wrote,

> This ethic of discipline, in both believing and unbelieving variants, was a moralism. It put discipline, self-control, the achieving of a high moral standard as the supreme goal. . . . Like all moralisms, it could come to seem too thin, too dry, concerned so exclusively with behaviour, discipline, control, that it left no space for some great élan or purpose which would transform our lives and take us out of the narrow focus on control. The obsession with getting myself to act right seems to leave no place for some overwhelmingly important goal or fulfillment, which is the one which gives point to my existence.[2]

We are wired for an "overwhelmingly important goal." Jesus described his overwhelmingly important goal as pleasing the Father. He said, "The one who sent me is with me; he has not left me alone, for I always do what pleases him" (John 8:29, NIV). Paul called his overwhelmingly important goal "the prize." He wrote, "The goal I pursue is the prize of God's upward call in Christ Jesus" (Phil 3:14). The upward call of Christ, pleasing the Father, and walking with the Spirit define the overwhelmingly important goal Jesus gave us. These all comprise what he meant by seeking the kingdom of God.

Acknowledging the existence of God's goal, the point of life, and setting it as our own is an important part of a healthy soul and congregational soul culture. Theologian Cornelius Plantinga calls it spiritual hygiene and describes it this way:

> Spiritual hygiene includes *ends* like these—goals, purposes, primary intended consequences. The point of our lives is not to get smart or to get

2. Charles Taylor, *A Secular Age* (Cambridge, MA: Belknap Press, 2007), 399.

> rich or even to get happy. The point is to discover God's purposes for us and make them our own. The point is to learn ways of loving God above all and our neighbor as ourselves and then to use these loves the way a golfer uses certain checkpoints to set up for a drive. The point is to be lined up right, to seek first the kingdom of God (Matt. 6:33), to try above all to increase the net amount of shalom in the world.[3]

Shalom is life as God intended. The Bible is a grand story of God giving and transforming life. Heaven is as God intends it. The world is marred by sin. We have vandalized shalom, yet God is working in lives and in churches to answer the prayer Jesus taught us to pray: "Your kingdom come, your will be done on earth, as it is in heaven" (Matt 6:10, NIV). Godly goals embody a cry for the kingdom.[4] Scripture suggests that we pursue godly goals at three levels. Life demonstrates that successful collaboratives work this way, validating how God designed us to collaborate with each other.

## The Goals Hierarchy

Angela Duckworth is a smart woman. She has a bachelor's degree in neurobiology from Harvard, a master's in neuroscience from Oxford, and a PhD in psychology from the University of Pennsylvania. In 2013 she became a MacArthur Fellow. This fellowship is known as the "Genius Grant." Duckworth is both fascinated and fascinating. She is drawn to how people work and work together. She believes in the shaping power of culture. Duckworth observes,

> Whether we realize it or not, the culture in which we live, and with which we identify, powerfully shapes just about every aspect of our being.
>
> By culture, I don't mean the geographic or political boundaries that divide one people from another as much as the invisible psychological boundaries separating *us* from *them*. At its core, a culture is defined by the shared norms and values of a group of people. In other words, a distinct

---

3. Cornelius Plantinga, Jr., *Not the Way It's Supposed to Be: A Breviary of Sin* (Grand Rapids, MI: Eerdmans, 1995), 37.

4. Houston Northwest Church models contextualization of this overwhelmingly important goal of Christ's kingdom through their "vision of making Houston more like Heaven." See Houston Northwest Church, "DNA & Beliefs," https://www.hnw.org/dna.

culture exists anytime a group of people are in consensus about how we do things around here and why.[5]

"Doing things" anticipates our next chapter's focus on practices. "Why" hearkens back to the previous chapter on values.[6] The bridge between values and practices is *goals*. As Duckworth advises corporate cultures, she often begins with ethnographic research to study their organization's goals. She once embedded with the Seattle Seahawks NFL team. Seahawks head coach Pete Carroll believes that "a clear, well-defined philosophy gives you the guidelines and boundaries that keep you on track."[7] Part of his philosophy and perhaps a way to understand it is to envision goals as a hierarchy. There is a singular top-level goal, a few mid-level goals connected to the top, and many low-level goals that contribute to the mid-level ones. We can sketch it out this way:

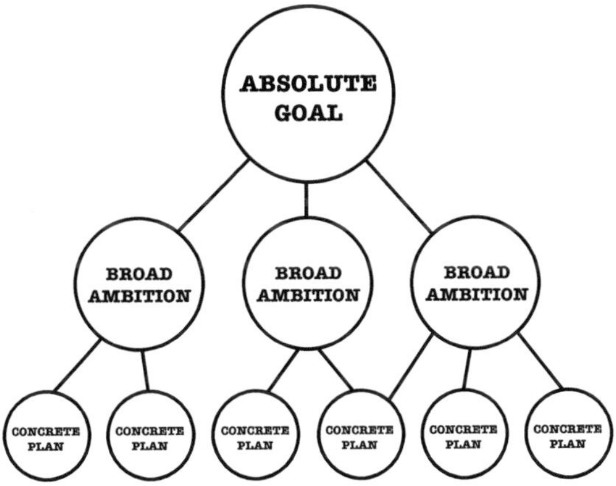


**Figure 1. Hierarchy of Goals**

This hierarchy is exactly how goal setting works in the New Testament. When we search the Bible, we see God leading Christians and the

5. Angela Duckworth, *Grit: The Power of Passion and Perseverance* (New York: Scribner, 2016), 244.

6. See Simon Sinek, "How Great Leaders Inspire Action," TEDxPuget Sound, https://www.ted.com/talks/simon_sinek_how_great_leaders_inspire_action/transcript?language=en; Simon Sinek, *Start with Why: How Great Leaders Inspire Everyone to Take Action* (New York: Portfolio, 2011).

7. Duckworth, *Grit*, 62.

church with an overwhelmingly important **Absolute Goal**. This Absolute Goal connects to a cluster of **Broad Ambitions**. These Broad Ambitions connect in turn to **Concrete Plans**. We might think of these as the ABCs of goal setting: Absolute, Broad, and Concrete. We can borrow Duckworth's bubble chart to conceptualize this hierarchy of goals, or we can think about them as stones in a pyramid:

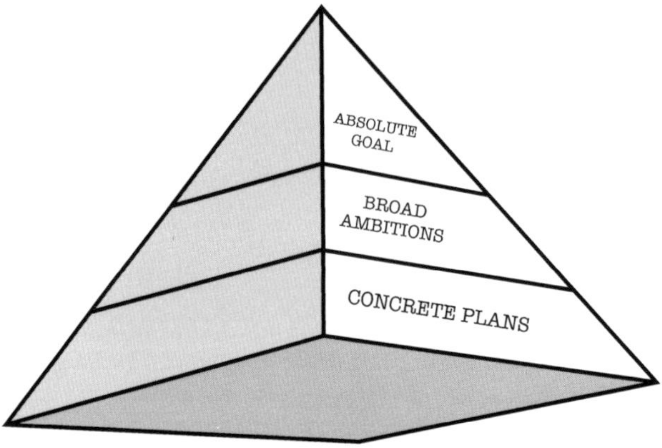


**Figure 2. An Ascending Pyramid**

## *Absolute Goal*

Seeking the kingdom of God means setting for ourselves God's overwhelmingly important absolute goal. Adopting this goal is the opposite of what the Gen-X crowd called "riding our own melt" (or going "your own way" as Fleetwood Mac celebrated for the Baby Boomers). When something is absolute, it has a way of simplifying reality. When God is God, we recognize all alternatives as not God. As E. Stanley Jones said, "The Kingdom and Jesus are the Way unqualified, the Way to think, to act, to feel, to be—in every relationship, in the individual and in the collective, for God and man. There are just two things in life—the Way or not the way."[8]

The kingdom of God is life with God, on God's terms. We experience God's reign in three tenses. It came in the past. We can experience it now in the present. It will be fully consummated in God's good future. William Abraham wrote, "God's rule had indeed begun in earnest; it is currently within the grasp of all who will reach out and receive it, and it will be brought to perfection in the great and manifest day of the

8. E. Stanley Jones, *The Unshakable Kingdom and the Unchanging Person* (E. Stanley Jones Foundation, 2017), 83.

Lord. . . . All three tenses are required if we are to begin to do justice to its inner complexity and dynamic."[9]

The kingdom came, and so we can receive it by faith. In Mark 10 people were bringing little children to Jesus so he could bless them.[10] This seems like a warm and wonderful thing, but the disciples apparently didn't think so. They glanced over the ministry menu and saw teaching, preaching, healing, raising the dead, lunch with crooks and prostitutes, conversations with theologians, and occasional retreats in the mountains. They did not see kid blessings, so they scolded the parents. While the parents nursed bruised egos, Jesus laid down some red letters: "Allow the children to come to me. Don't forbid them, because God's kingdom belongs to people like these children. I assure you that whoever doesn't welcome God's kingdom like a child will never enter it" (Mark 10:14-15).

Children are vulnerable and needy. They can't survive on their own. Almost every civilization has special laws to protect them. We receive like a child when we recognize our inability to acquire what we need the most on our own. We can't purchase, earn, barter, or win life with God. We can only receive it as a gift. And God delights in giving it. Jesus said in Luke 12:32, "Don't be afraid, little flock, because your Father delights in giving you the kingdom." This is where our life with God begins both as individual Christ followers and as his constituted church. This is how Christ becomes our life. This is how we are saved: "You are saved by God's grace because of your faith. This salvation is God's gift. It's not something you possessed. It's not something you did that you can be proud of. Instead, we are God's accomplishment, created in Christ Jesus to do good things. God planned for these things to be the way that we live our lives" (Eph 2:8-10). We can set life-giving plans and goals because God had a plan. God planned our way of life. Our plans can *synchronize* with God's plans.

Setting goals and making plans is a huge part of healthy church culture. We need to make sure that the top of the pyramid is a commitment to reminding one another over and over that the goal is seeking the kingdom, which we must first receive as gift. A congregation with the gospel at the top is prepared to set wise goals.

---

9. William J. Abraham, *The Logic of Evangelism* (Grand Rapids, MI: Eerdmans, 1989), 32.

10. Justin Earley rightly highlights the holy ambition of the parents in bringing these children to Jesus. See his *Habits of the Household: Practicing the Story of God in Everyday Family Rhythms* (Grand Rapids, MI: Zondervan, 2021), 118.

As we seek the kingdom of God, we must also remember that the kingdom is a present reality experienced in a gritty, earthy way. The kingdom petition of the Lord's Prayer gets answered when we walk in the Spirit of God and live by the word of Christ. Paul said in 2 Corinthians 3:17, "The Lord is the Spirit, and where the Lord's Spirit is there is freedom." The free Christian is bound by the liberating plan of God. We can know and enjoy this freedom through the Spirit.

This freedom is not trite or triumphalist. It is both sober and hopeful. The joy this liberty brings is sometimes a melancholy joy. It contends with limitations that come with being on earth and not in heaven. It's not complete or safe, but it is good. Barth insightfully put it this way:

> It is true enough that man may presently know and enjoy this freedom through the abiding Spirit of the Father and the Son only in spite of sin, flesh, and death; in spite of the world, his earthly anxiety and his worldly nature; and in spite of himself in his persistent temptation. This however, does not prevent man from being enabled to know and to live out this freedom in incomparable and inexhaustible joy, limited as his own awareness may be.[11]

We can experience the kingdom now and need to make it our goal to do so. This overwhelmingly important Absolute Goal should animate all of Christ's churches.

We also need to remind ourselves that the promise of the Parousia, Christ's second coming, is as real as the promise of the Spirit's presence. It's as sure as resurrection. One day our awareness will be without limit. We will see. The vision of Isaiah 65 and Revelation 22 will become reality. We will walk by sight and not faith. This horizon of hope is a key element in godly goal-setting. May we pursue the things that will remain in God's good future.

## *Broad Ambitions*

Mid-level goals are broad category goals. They are Broad Ambitions that drive toward the overwhelmingly important Absolute Goal. When we read the Gospels, we see that Jesus had some Broad Ambitions. It's hard

---

11. Karl Barth, *The Humanity of God* (Louisville: Westminster John Knox, 1960), 78–79. Recall here the full text of Reinhold Niebuhr's "Serenity Prayer" from chapter 3 with its petition to be "reasonably happy in this life and supremely happy with Him forever and ever in the next."

for many of us to hear the words *Jesus* and *ambition* in the same sentence without singing a little Michael W. Smith, circa 1988. Go ahead, sing along: "Nobody knew His secret ambition, nobody knew His claim to fame . . . ."[12] This line is catchy but theologically debatable. We won't quarrel over it now; let's just agree that we *now* know both Jesus's ambitions and his claim to fame. He came to give us life in the kingdom of God. He came to be human as God intended. During his earthly ministry, Jesus's acts revealed what his ambitions were. Jesus is a model for true human life. He showed us what an icon of God looks like. Jonathan Martin asks, "What if Jesus were God's prototype for a whole new way of being human?"[13]

Acts 10:38 is a great synthesis statement of the way Jesus lived as the image of God. He planned his work and worked his plan. Luke wrote, "You know about Jesus of Nazareth, whom God anointed with the Holy Spirit and endowed with power. Jesus traveled around doing good and healing everyone oppressed by the devil because God was with him." Jesus was about pleasing the Father. He lived this out in worship, work, and witness.

### *Worship*

God was with Jesus. We can equally say that Jesus was with God. Acts 10:38 is one of the many verses that pressed the church to articulate the doctrine of the Trinity. We may say that adoration is at the core of God's "God-ness." God is adoring love. Jesus spent time with the Father. He worshiped corporately many times, even with people who meant him grave ill (perhaps we should let this put some of our own congregational drama in perspective). He retreated to spend extended times in personal prayer and worship. He sought the Father in a small group. Worship was a second-level goal connected to Jesus's ultimate goal of pleasing the Father.

Worship is a fixed and given goal for all God's people for all times. If we live pursuing the kingdom of God, we will prioritize worshiping God. The Broad Ambition to worship incorporates both personal and corporate aspects of adoring God. One of the finest definitions of worship comes from Judson Cornwall. He said, "Worship is a response. The simplest definition

---

12. Michael W. Smith, Wayne Kirkpatrick, and Amy Grant, "Secret Ambition," performed by Michael W. Smith, track 2 on *i 2 (EYE)*, 1988.

13. Jonathan Martin, *Prototype: What Happens When You Discover You're More Like Jesus than You Think* (Carol Stream, IL: Tyndale Momentum, 2013), 18. Millennial readers might notice an echo of Switchfoot's "new way to be human" here. See Jon Foreman and Douglas Kaine McKelvey, "New Way to Be Human," performed by Switchfoot, track 1 on *New Way to Be Human*, 1999.

of worship is 'love responding to love.' Until there is an awareness of God's love flowing into our lives, there is nothing to respond to. Worship, then, requires an acquaintance with the object of our affection."[14] We see again how the ingredients of soul culture interact; our *goal* to worship is conditioned by theological *beliefs* and Christlike *attitudes*.

### *Work*

Jesus "traveled around doing good" (Acts 10:38). Jesus was a working man, consistent with the biblical portrait of work as one of God's good gifts from creation.[15] He grew up at Joseph's side doing physical labor. Perhaps he was part of the labor force that rebuilt Sepphoris, the great city on a hill. When Jesus shifted to a season of public ministry, supported by the sacrificial gifts of grateful people, he began it with calluses on his hands. Jesus was a Messiah with a blue-collar work ethic. His service to the Father benefited those around him. His labors were a blessing. Diligent work for God's glory and other people's blessing is a mark of godly goals. Nehemiah 4:6 celebrates how God's people "had a mind to work" (ESV). Do we plan to work, or are we just hoping for things to happen in life and ministry?

I (Matt) once served as the pastor of Truitt Memorial Baptist Church in Pearl, Mississippi. Truitt Memorial was a neighborhood church just outside Jackson proper. The pastor who shaped the culture at Truitt the most was a godly man named J. L. Reeves. Known affectionately as Brother Reeves, he worked the dough of soul culture at Truitt Memorial for half a century. When I became pastor, I studied his sermon cassettes to learn about what made him tick. In one of the messages, Reeves said, "Any church that honors Christ as its head will do some good in a community." He said it almost as an observation, a given, but I heard it as a promise. Christ, church, and community—these words summarized and guided our goals. We put Brother Reeves's quote on posters and t-shirts, and it became something of a watchword. It helped give focus to a season of congregational renewal. It kept us from paternalistic "do-gooderism" by rooting our work in the Lordship of Christ. It kept us from becoming isolationists by recognizing that the Spirit of Christ in our midst naturally—or shall we say supernaturally—compels us to "work for the good of all . . . and especially for those in the household of faith" (Gal 6:10). Working for the good of all

---

14. Judson Cornwall, *Incense and Insurrection: God's Definitive Answer to Rebellion: Worship* (Shippensburg, PA: Destiny Image Publishers, 1995), 7.

15. See Earley, *Habits of the Household*, 148.

as God gives us the opportunity is a Broad Ambition every church should have. Jesus modeled it, and his presence in our midst animates it.

### *Witness*

Mark 1:14 reads, "After John was arrested, Jesus came into Galilee announcing God's good news, saying, 'Now is the time! Here comes God's kingdom! Change your hearts and lives, and trust this good news!'" A vital part of Jesus's "doing good" was his commitment to announce verbally the favor of God. He told people about life with God and how they could get in on it. He modeled this proclamation for his disciples. He prepared them to do it as well and gave them opportunities to share the message. One of the fixed Broad Ambitions God has placed on local congregations is the goal of sharing good news.

Paul described the goal of witness this way: "So we are ambassadors who represent Christ. God is negotiating with you through us. We beg you as Christ's representatives, 'Be reconciled to God!'" (2 Cor 5:20). Every local church is a company of ambassadors, a diplomatic corps. We live in the world with a dual identity and have a fiduciary responsibility to the power that sends us. We live in the world, not of it, but for God and for the world.

We have a coworker named Cecil Dunham. Cecil is a spry octogenarian and the best storyteller on our church staff. Cecil has always had a bunch of interesting friends. One of them was once part of a delegation that delivered Texas barbeque to Sweden. At that time, the US Ambassador to Sweden was another of Cecil's friends, the Texan Lyndon Olson. Ambassador Olson thought a little imported Texas love could do wonders for international relations. Who's to argue with that? Ambassadors represent their home country and do official business as delegated authorities. The church has a delegated authority to make God's appeal. To bring some of heaven to earth. To beg on God's behalf. How stunning is that?

It is fashionable now to attribute to Francis of Assisi the line, "Preach the gospel at all times; when necessary, use words." The major problem with doing so is that it is highly unlikely Francis ever said such a thing. It certainly doesn't square with his life. The man preached to birds and wolves! He talked of God's love all the time. The notion of a wordless gospel makes as much sense as saying, "Feed the hungry at all times; when necessary, use food."

We see the Broad Ambitions of worship, work, and witness in Jesus's life. These abide as Broad Ambitions given for each congregation. Some churches use the "Saddleback 5" to articulate Broad Ambitions of worship, discipleship, fellowship, service, and witness.[16] These five categories slightly elaborate the threefold worship, work, and witness. These Broad Ambitions are for all congregations, in every setting, for all time.

### *Congregational Wisdom*

We also believe that each congregation becomes stewards of unique Broad Ambitions that God distributes throughout the church. When I became pastor of First Baptist Church Waco in 2010, I began as an encourager and ethnographer. The ethnography helped us discern the unique contributions our congregation could make in the community. We sought wisdom to discover the unique shape of our worship, work, and witness for our own time and place. Here are some of the things we did:

- Angel of the Lord Questions: The angel of the Lord asked Hagar, "Where did you come from and where are you going?" (Gen 16:8). We met with individuals and groups and asked them to answer these questions. Like Hagar, they felt seen (see Gen 16:13), and they also gave many important data points on the unique soul culture that is FBC Waco.
- The Rod of God: We would meet with groups and pass around a wooden staff. We'd tell people that it carried the power to makes things happen. We would then ask them what they would do with it.
- Decades of Membership: During church-wide fellowships, we taped large pieces of butcher paper on the wall. We labeled them by decade going back to the arrival of our longest-tenured members. We then asked participants to find the decade when they joined the church and scribble down their reason(s) why. This exercise helped identify themes that have been part of the congregation's ethos since its beginning.
- Asset Mapping: Heather Mustain came to us as a resident from Baylor's Diana Garland School of Social Work. She had been trained in asset-based community development (ABCD).[17] We surveyed FBC Waco members and mapped our own assets. Asset mapping helped us identify our "loaves and fishes" so we could offer them to Jesus.

---

16. See Rick Warren, *The Purpose Driven Life* (Grand Rapids, MI: Zondervan, 2002).

17. Luther K. Snow, *The Power of Asset Mapping: How Your Congregation Can Act on Its Gifts* (Herndon, VA: The Alban Institute, 2004) is a helpful introduction to this practice.

• Interviews and Small Talk: No leadership skill is more important than listening. What are the people saying? What is the Spirit saying to and through them?

At the end of several months of listening and discerning, we saw that the congregation was ambitious to be a Scripture-loving people. They wanted to serve the mission of God in the world. They desired for the membership to take responsibility for the vitality of the congregation. They wanted to "do church" across our multiple generations. They recognized that our downtown location required a ministry that was regional in nature. The church spoke to longstanding commitments to Christian education at the university and seminary level. Part of the broad ambitions for First Baptist Waco must include education. The church recognized that we are an eclectic bunch. Ministry style and worship practice must draw from many sources.

When a church is in a season of transition, discerning the unique callings on a congregation needs to be a high priority. Without this step, new leaders tend to import values and ambitions that may not fit just right. First Baptist Church Waco can't function like a suburban megachurch, and a suburban megachurch probably shouldn't do ministry exactly like us. David refused to wear Saul's armor, and so should we.

As a church goes from season to season, a solid sense of its Broad Ambitions helps the church make ministry decisions consistent with a healthy congregational identity. "What should we do?" needs to be preceded by "Who has God called us to be?" We know that we are to seek the kingdom of God together. This is the Absolute Goal. Our Broad Ambitions help us make sense of how that works in our particular part of the world.

## *Concrete Plans*

FBC Waco once had a Scottish pastor named Peter McLeod. He often remarked, "Let's concretize this." He rolled the "r" so hard that it all but made the admonition a done deal. Who could resist? Concrete Plans are the third level of congregational goals. The kingdom of God is every congregation's overwhelmingly important Absolute Goal. It is the top of the pyramid. The large stones in the middle of the pyramid are the Broad Ambitions that support the top. God-given congregational values drive these ambitions and help the church understand identity and communicate direction. The many stones at the base of the pyramid are the Concrete

Plans churches make in leadership gatherings, staff meetings, and church conferences.

We have examples of Concrete Plans in Scripture. One illustrative text is 1 Corinthians 16:5-9:

> I'll come to you after I go through Macedonia, and because I'm going through Macedonia, I may stay with you or even spend the winter there in Corinth so that you can send me on my way to wherever I'm off to next. I don't want to make a quick visit to you, since I hope to spend some time with you if the Lord lets it happen. I'll stay here in Ephesus until the Festival of Pentecost. In spite of the fact that there are many opponents, a big and productive opportunity has opened up for my mission here.

Notice how Paul talked about specific, time-bound goals. He operated on inspired ideas and demonstrated initiative, but he was humble in holding his plans. Everything was contingent on the will of God. He was convinced that God leads by revelation and was confident God will reveal God's will to ordinary, sometimes even immature, Christians.

One of the main ways Paul discerned directions and made plans was through open doors of opportunity. The substantial and fascinating Baptist theologian James McClendon once wrote,

> How, then, does God who is Spirit work? Running through the New Testament is the image of a door. It can represent access of the missionaries to their task (2 Cor. 2:2). Yet that door that admits the missionaries opens for new believers as well (Acts 14:27), giving them access to the realm the missionaries proclaim. The door image is consummate in Revelation 3:8, where the "open door which no one can shut" means God-given access to the eschatological glory—the door to the great banquet feast of heaven.[18]

Paul understood that he represented and proclaimed a "realm." He was an ambassador of the kingdom of heaven. The King still opens doors no one can close. This sanctifies what appears so ordinary. It certainly does not mean ministry will be easy or free of opposition. It does mean that we are certainly not alone in the world. God is God, and part of working the dough of congregational soul culture is submitting our plans to God

---

18. James Wm. McClendon, Jr., *Doctrine*, vol. 2 of *Systematic Theology* (Nashville: Abingdon, 1994), 428–29.

and recognizing that planning and calendar work is as holy as singing, preaching, and praying.

Jesus taught us to pray, "your kingdom come, your will be done, on earth as it is in heaven" (Matt 6:10, NIV). If we can see ourselves standing at the base of a pyramid looking up at the overwhelmingly important Absolute Goal of seeking the kingdom, perhaps we can also imagine God looking down. God would likely turn the image upside down and place our point for living at the bottom. God might turn our pyramid into a funnel. The kingdom's Absolute Goal would now be at the bottom, with Broad Ambitions and Concrete Plans above. Into this funnel God, who inspired all that is in it, would pour God's own goodness and grace to push kingdom dynamics into real-life situations. God's love flows downward!

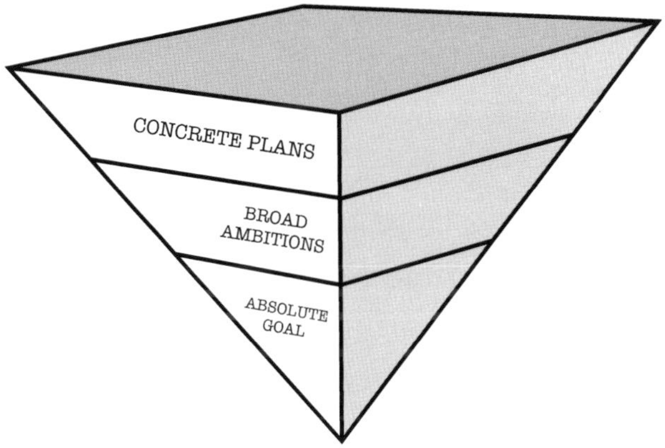


**Figure 3. A Descending Funnel**

Martin Luther said, "Rather than seeking its own good, the love of God flows forth and bestows good."[19] In a similar way Thomas Smail said, "The gospel of the ascended Lord who pours out his gifts is also the gospel of the humiliated Servant who pours out his blood."[20] We serve a God of grace and glory. We seek the prize of the upward call. God humbly draws near on earth. God comes down. This union of earth and heaven is what goals are all about.

19. Martin Luther, *Career of the Reformer*, vol. 31 of *Luther's Works* (Philadelphia: Fortress, 1999), 57–58.

20. Thomas A. Smail, *Reflected Glory: The Spirit in Christ and Christians* (Grand Rapids, MI: Eerdmans, 1975), 60.

## Conclusion

Life has a point. This is a Christian conviction. Because it is true, we need to be goal-oriented in our individual lives and in our congregations. It is important for us to take our guidance from Scripture and be discerning about borrowing from other sources because we can be tempted to set goals that do not reflect God's priorities. We're tempted to imagine the way we want things to be and forget that Christ is the head of the church. We need to resign once and for all from being God. When we deal with goals and vision in the church, we must keep before us the theological conviction that we are followers before we are leaders. Having a vision uncoupled from God's is not only misguided; it is damaging.

In his wonderful work *Life Together*, Dietrich Bonhoeffer confronted this tendency head on. He told his underground seminary community,

> Every human wish dream that is injected into the Christian community is a hindrance to genuine community and must be banished if genuine community is to survive. He who loves his dream of community more than the Christian community itself becomes a destroyer of the latter, even though his personal intentions may be ever so honest and earnest and sacrificial.
>
> God hates visionary dreaming; it makes the dreamer proud and pretentious. The man who fashions a visionary ideal of community demands that it be realized by God, by others, and by himself. He enters the community of Christians with his demands, sets up his own law, and judges the brethren and God Himself accordingly.[21]

We live out our Christian lives in a real church and worship the God that is God. Godly goal-setting is not daydreaming in Sunday clothes.

Our goals and our vision must be rooted in God's goals and vision. Therefore, beliefs, attitudes, and values must be part of the mix when we set goals. Those three things free goals from both futility and idolatry.

Many thoughtful Christians have called Leonard Sweet a visionary, even a seer. I am sure the Methodist bishop who asked him about his vision was therefore shocked when Sweet said, "Sir, *I* don't have a vision. . . . I'm

---

21. Dietrich Bonhoeffer, *Life Together* (San Francisco: Harper San Francisco, 1954), 27.

following a vision, but it's not my vision. The vision is Jesus. I grew up singing a hymn I take literally: 'Be Thou My Vision, O Lord of my life.'"[22]

The Absolute Goal is Jesus and his Way, the kingdom. Our Broad Ambitions and Concrete Plans must serve that Absolute Goal. We can fix our eyes on the Absolute, the eternal, and look for marks of the eternal on our daily, weekly, monthly, and yearly plans.

Chapter 5

# Goals

**Questions for Further Reflection**

1. Type "what's the point" into your search engine of choice. What are the first three recommendations that appear?

   (1)

   (2)

   (3)

How do you answer, "What's the point?"

2. In the movie *Reality Bites*, Troy describes the moment when he "realized that the shell was empty," when the place he looked for answers came up short. Have you had a similar moment of crisis or disillusionment? How did you respond?

3. Read through the book of Ecclesiastes, or at least chapters 1–2 and 12. The Philosopher/Preacher explores pleasures of luxury, power, knowledge, and achievement and finds them all wanting. Which one(s) are most tempting for you? Do they fully satisfy or disappoint?

Ecclesiastes concludes, "So this is the end of the matter; all has been heard. Worship God and keep God's commandments because this is what everyone must do" (12:13).

4. Do you have an "overwhelmingly important goal"? How do you describe it in your own words?

5. Absolute goals serve to simplify reality. Are there areas of your life that need simplification?

22. Leonard Sweet, *Nudge: Awakening Each Other to the God Who's Already There* (Colorado Springs: David C. Cook, 2010), 209.

6. Reflect on Judson Cornwall's definition of worship as "love responding to love."

• How does this *goal* (and ultimately *practice*) interact with your *beliefs*?

______________________________________________

______________________________________________

______________________________________________

______________________________________________

______________________________________________

• How about your *attitudes*?

______________________________________________

______________________________________________

______________________________________________

______________________________________________

______________________________________________

7. Spend a few minutes prayerfully completing this pyramid diagram containing your personal Absolute Goal, Broad Ambitions, and Concrete Plans. What goals animate your life?

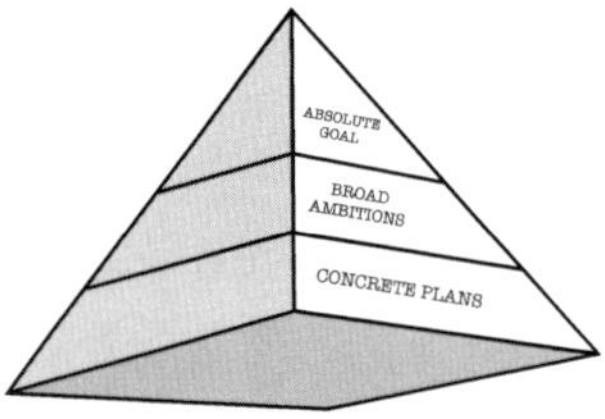


*Figure 2.* An Ascending Pyramid

# Chapter 5: Goals

## *Group Discussion Guide*

Broad ambitions for every healthy church include worship, work, and witness. These wide priorities orient us and mutually reinforce one another. Think of them as three legs of a stool.

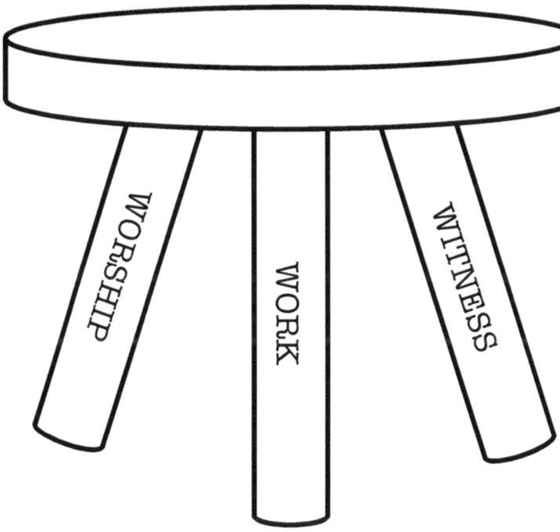


**Figure 4. The Church's Broad Ambitions**

1. How does your church engage each one of these? *(You may want to list responses on a whiteboard or flip chart.)*
    - Worship
    - Work
    - Witness

2. Is your church particularly strong in one of these three categories?

3. Is there an area of relative weakness?

4. Are there any regular practices of your church (or in your personal life) that don't fit within any of these three categories? If so, how do you respond? *(Discuss this question in small groups and then share responses.)*

5. List the ways that your congregation verbally proclaims the good news of Jesus.

6. Lesslie Newbigin's modes of mission are helpful here.[23] Newbigin describes the church bearing witness to the good news of Christ in three primary ways:

- The church as alternative community (a largely nonverbal witness; the simple fact of the church sharing life with one another as the church)
- Church members' personal witness in daily activity (individuals' verbal testimony 24/7, at soccer practice, in the grocery line, with coworkers, etc.)
- Organized, planned corporate witness (short- or long-term mission trips, deliberately evangelistic events, door-to-door testimony, etc.)

7. Godly work for the good of others navigates the narrow path between two ditches, paternalistic "do-gooderism" on one side and isolationism on the other. Which one is more tempting for your church? How do you resist this temptation with an ambition for godly work?

**Congregational Ethnography Activities**

• Angel of the Lord Questions: Divide into small groups and ask the "Angel of the Lord questions" from Genesis 16:8: "Where did you come from and where are you going?" Encourage both personal and congregational answers. Reconvene and share responses with the whole group.

• The Rod of God: Return to small groups and try the "Rod of God" exercise. Pass around a wooden staff (or any other item, really!). Tell participants that this item carries the power to make things happen. What would they like to change?

• Decades of Membership: Post large pieces of butcher paper around the room labeled with decades going back to the arrival of your church's longest-tenured members. Ask participants to find the decade when they joined the church and write down their reason(s) for joining. After everyone

---

23. Lesslie Newbigin, *Truth to Tell: The Gospel as Public Truth* (Grand Rapids, MI: Eerdmans, 1991); see also Newbigin, *The Gospel in a Pluralist Society* (Grand Rapids, MI: Eerdmans, 1989); Michael W. Goheen, *The Church and Its Vocation: Lesslie Newbigin's Missionary Ecclesiology* (Grand Rapids, MI: Baker Academic, 2018).

has recorded their responses, discuss them together. Pay attention to places of long-term continuity and to any significant changes.

• Asset Mapping: Brainstorm the distinct assets of your church congregation. Think in terms of both material resources and skills (goods and services). How could the church bring these assets to bear to serve one another and the community?[24]

1. What wisdom do these four ethnographic exercises provide to help discern the Broad Ambitions specific to your congregation and context? What particular expressions of worship, work, and witness do they suggest?

2. Does your church have a formalized process for goal-setting?
    - When does it occur?
    - Who participates?
    - How are goals communicated and then implemented?
    - How are they evaluated?

3. We suggest a hierarchy of goals including an Absolute Goal, Broad Ambitions, and Concrete Plans.
    - Which level of goal setting comes most readily for your church?
    - Which one is most challenging?

4. We argue in this chapter that "planning and calendar work is as holy as singing, preaching, and praying." Does your church honor this sort of work that gives concrete expression to its goals?

5. Goals function on daily, weekly, monthly, and yearly rhythms (and beyond!). List some goals (current or intended) for each of these time horizons on a whiteboard or flip chart.

6. Read Mark 10:13-16 together. Jesus's disciples scolded parents because they didn't recognize blessing children on the "ministry menu."
    - How do we respond when unforeseen ministry opportunities arise?
    - How do we discern whether to engage an unanticipated opportunity or pass it by?

---

24. For more guidance here, see Luther K. Snow, *The Power of Asset Mapping: How Your Congregation Can Act on Its Gifts* (Herndon, VA: The Alban Institute, 2004).

# 6. Practices

> *Whatever you do, whether in speech or action, do it all in the name of the Lord Jesus and give thanks to God the Father through him.*
>
> Colossians 3:17

> *You must be doers of the word and not only hearers who mislead themselves.*
>
> James 1:22

My father was a builder. Tim Snowden built buildings and sons and a life with our mother. His memory is an opportunity for all of us to whisper prayers of gratitude to the giver of good gifts. Many of my memories are set on construction sites.

When I was a kid, the O. L. Snowden and Sons Construction company was low bidder on a bread factory renovation project. Dad was overseer for the crew that worked on Smith's Sunbeam Bread. One of my most vivid recollections of visiting that site is the fresh-baked bread. The company would sell us loaves of hot, unsliced sandwich bread before they had even completed their conveyor belt journeys. Most of the construction workers I grew up around had never heard of the gluten-free life. They loved that warm sandwich bread. They even began bringing wheels of margarine wrapped in wax paper inside their Igloo coolers, and they converted the change from their cupholders into piping hot loaves of baked goodness. Boring white bread is pretty amazing before you cut it up, cool it down, wrap it in plastic, and ship it to Winn-Dixie.

Smith's Sunbeam was known for bread. Smith's was the company; bread was the product. Bread was sold and bought. You could handle, see, smell, and taste the bread. Without the bread there was no . . . well, bread. But Smith's Sunbeam was more than bread. It was gears and cranks, belts and hoses. It was a labor crew and engineers. It was accountants and contracts, processes and methods. It was history and a genesis story, leadership and lessons. Smith's was a culture, and Sunbeam bread was its manifestation.

Church practices are the things a church does that are seen, heard, smelled, touched, and tasted. They are the things a congregation does. Some recur regularly. We pray and read the Scripture daily. We gather for worship each week on the Lord's Day. Monthly practices give rhythm to our church calendars, and annual celebrations mark the incarnation, the resurrection, and the gift of the Holy Spirit. Other practices are more occasional; they arise in response to particular opportunities or challenges. Some are divine appointments that come only once. Whatever their schedule, all of these practices emerge from a host of cultural realities, just like the Smith's Sunbeam Bread Company. Christian practices are the bread produced as we knead the dough composed of our beliefs, attitudes, values, and goals.

Colossians 3:17 says, "Whatever you do, whether in speech or action, do it all in the name of the Lord Jesus and give thanks to God the Father through him." Practices, simply defined, are *whatever we do*. Colossians 3:1-16 is a comprehensive call to root our speech and action in all the elements of godly congregational soul culture. All systems are firing in this brief apostolic admonition that deals with goals, values, attitudes, and beliefs.

## Kneading the Dough

### *Goals*

Paul wrote, "Therefore, if you were raised with Christ, look for things that are above where Christ is sitting at God's right side" (Col 3:1). The ultimate and overwhelmingly important congregational goal of seeking the kingdom of God springs from Christ's empty tomb. Theologian James McClendon used an odd and beautiful phrase to describe the ethical speech and action of the church in the world. He spoke of the "Easter Phalanx." McClendon admitted, "'Easter Phalanx' may seem a queer metaphor coming from an announced pacifist."[1] Phalanx is a warring word. In ancient Greece where the term arose, it referred "to a nearly invulnerable unit" of soldiers grouped so tightly that they could challenge any enemy.[2] Alexander the Great used the phalanx to conquer the world. The empty tomb opens the possibility of a phalanx of the baptized, linked together and pursuing the same great goals.

1. James Wm. McClendon, Jr., *Ethics*, vol. 1 of *Systematic Theology*, rev. ed. (Nashville: Abingdon Press, 2002), 265.

2. Ibid.

Resurrection grace and the pursuit of things above must touch the church's practices. If godly goals do not animate church practices, we lose our distinctive witness in the world. When this happens, the church enters a dangerous position with threats on both sides. On one side the church is vulnerable to losing spiritual vitality and relevance as it compromises core beliefs. It becomes the Optimist Club with better music, merely one more helping organization among the many. This tendency may seem benign, but the corporate sins of omission that it generates will cause lasting damage.

The danger on the other flank is the threat of secular powers coopting the church and using it to advance causes and personalities contrary to the way of Christ. The desire to be in inner circles of power and influence is strong indeed. In C. S. Lewis's brilliant talk "The Inner Ring,"[3] he argues that the desire to be (in Lin-Manuel Miranda's memorable words) "in the room where it happens" warps the soul.[4] Lewis wrote, "Of all passions the passion for the Inner Ring is most skillful in making a man who is not yet a very bad man do very bad things."[5] This drive is as common as table salt and usually rooted in greed or fear. It clouds vision and warps both speech and action.

It also makes us foolish. Cormac McCarthy places an incredible observation on the lips of a New Orleans private investigator in his novel *The Passenger*. The PI looks at his client and says, "When smart people do dumb things it's usually due to one of two things. The two things are greed and fear. They want something they're not supposed to have, or they've done something they weren't supposed to do. In either case they've usually fastened on to a set of beliefs that are supportive of their state of mind but at odds with reality."[6] When we as Christians and congregations quit looking for the things where Christ is sitting above, we fasten on to other goals that put us at odds with Easter reality. We then say and do things that do not make sense for a people raised with Jesus.

Living according to our Easter goal sets liberating limits for the church. Unlimited options are quite a curse. Walker Percy penned a latter-day beatitude in his novel *The Last Gentleman*, where he quipped, "Lucky is the

---

3. C. S. Lewis, "The Inner Ring," in *The Weight of Glory* (New York: HarperOne, 2001), 141–57.

4. Lin-Manuel Miranda, "The Room Where It Happens," recorded 2015, track 28 on *Hamilton: An American Musical (Original Broadway Cast Recording)*, 2015.

5. Lewis, "Inner Ring," 154.

6. Cormac McCarthy, *The Passenger* (New York: Knopf, 2022), 269.

man who does not secretly believe that every possibility is open to him."[7] As Christians we simply are not free to choose our own adventure. The gospel of God constrains us. Karl Barth once commented, "[The] divine Source sets the limit to the centrifugal action. . . . Those who look to it as the 'one thing' see that limit and begin to respect it."[8] When we ground our action and speech in the goal of seeking the kingdom of God, we show God that we respect the divine limits. Then our ministry takes on force and focus.

We both make our homes in Texas but come from the Southeast. Both of us therefore cross the Mississippi River from time to time. Honestly, we cross quite a few rivers that divide us from loved ones. Crossing the Mississippi is always a humbling and awe-inspiring experience. The river is vast and strong. It has occasioned the spilling of blood, the battle of Vicksburg being one of the darkest moments in our nation's history. It has inspired songs and stories. The river is still a major part of the American economy. The Mississippi River without her banks would be the world's most ghastly swamp. Goals are to practices what banks are to rivers.

### *Values*

Colossians 3:4 reads, "When Christ, who is your life, is revealed, then you also will be revealed with him in glory." What a remarkable way to describe Christ: "your life." This description is worthy of some deep reflection. When a person acts in a shallow way that suggests they are grasping for purpose, someone else often burns them with the salty comment, "Get a life." Life is synonymous with what we value most, our telos. Partners and parents sometimes say to their beloveds, "You are my life." When Paul identified Christ as the Colossian Christians' life, he was saying that Jesus was what they valued the most. They had thrown all their hopes into Jesus's lap. He was the answer to their deepest question. He was their life.

Every Christian and every congregation must settle the life question. What is our reason for existence? We should regularly return to the hymn of Christ in Colossians 1:15-18:

> The Son is the image of the invisible God,
> the one who is first over all creation,

---

7. Walker Percy, *The Last Gentleman* (New York: Picador, 1966), 4.

8. Karl Barth, *The Epistle to the Philippians*, trans. James W. Leitch (Richmond, VA: John Knox Press, 1962), 54.

Because all things were created by him:
both in the heavens and on earth,
the things that are visible and the things that are invisible.
Whether they are thrones or powers,
or rulers or authorities,
all things were created through him and for him.

He existed before all things,
and all things are held together in him.

He is the head of the body, the church,
who is the beginning,
the one who is firstborn from among the dead
so that he might occupy the first place in everything.

Christ made it all and deserves to be first in every category. Do we value him that way? Is he our life? Is he yours?

### *Attitude*

Speech and action can never be divorced from attitude. Paul spills most of his ink imploring the Colossian believers to strip off their old sinful attitudes and carefully put on new godly attitudes. Colossians 3:5-15 includes a murderer's row of devilish attitudes that are as contemporary as the daily news. Paul lists sexual immorality, moral corruption, lust, evil desires, greed, anger, rage, malice, slander, obscene language, and lies.

I once did a personal experiment concerning the state of journalism. I spent a month listing to NPR, reading the *Wall Street Journal*, and watching Tucker Carlson. I determined that we live in at least three different worlds, all of which share the same problems. If you eliminated the vices listed in Colossians 3, Left, Right, and Center would have absolutely nothing to talk about. Sinful attitudes drive the winds of war and provide fodder for whispered gossip. Sinful attitudes are common as pigs' tracks and about as helpful. Paul calls us to embrace instead the attitudes of God's kingdom.

Compassion, kindness, humility, gentleness, patience, tolerance, forgiveness, love, peace, and thankfulness define God's people.[9] God will not allow us to shortchange goodness on the way to greatness. God wants

9. Note the similarities between these attitudes from Colossians 3 and the fruit of the Spirit listed in Galatians 5:22-23.

us to wrap ourselves in the values of Jesus and adopt an attitude consistent with his.

One of the finest men I've ever known was Red Covington. Red was an orthopedic surgeon and the longtime team doctor for the Baylor football team. When Red was a young man, the First Baptist Church of Waco called a young pastor named Peter McLeod. Ed Martin, an old church leader, decided Peter needed a friend, so he went to Red. He told him, "Red, I'm old. I can't be this man's friend, but every pastor needs a friend. You do that." And he did. Red and Peter became friends, and they loved one another until death parted them.

When I became the pastor of FBC Waco, Red went to some guys my age. One of them was Ed Martin's grandson Martin Starr. Red gave them all Ed's speech: "I am too old to be this man's friend, but every pastor needs a friend. You must do that." Those men have been my friends for a dozen years. In those years we have buried our fathers and raised our children. This charge from Red may be one of the greatest gifts in my life. I am forever humbled by it and thankful for it.

When Red died, I struggled through his funeral service. I wept like a child. The only thing I remember saying was, "On his way to becoming great, Red Covington decided to be good." Good he was. The gospel of God shaped his attitude. Red's speech and action conformed to the attitude of Jesus. We must decide to be good if we endeavor to become great. Attitudes drive speech and action. We need the attitudes of Christ in order for our practices to reflect the kingdom of God.

## *Beliefs*

Colossians 3:16 is bold. It says, "The word of Christ must live in you richly. Teach and warn each other with all wisdom by singing psalms, hymns, and spiritual songs. Sing to God with gratitude in your hearts." Christian theology is the atmosphere in which the church dwells. We affirm and proclaim the word of Christ, and then we turn it into poetry and song. From at least the fifth century, the church has recognized that what we pray and sing in worship reflects our most sincerely held doctrine.[10] We hum and pray our beliefs. Many of us have witnessed how aging saints cling to their sung beliefs and receive encouragement from them long after the

10. Prosper of Aquitaine, a fifth-century disciple of Augustine of Hippo, coined the Latin phrase *lex orandi, lex credendi,* translated "the law of praying [is] the law of believing."

rest of their memories have passed. The word of Christ is the iron spine of our common life. Speech and action emerge from godly beliefs, the faith committed to the body of Christ.

### *Practices*

When all the systems fire correctly, effective Christian practices result from a godly congregational culture. When it comes to igniting practices, Colossians 3:17 has no rival. This text says, "Whatever you do, whether in speech or action, do it all in the name of the Lord Jesus and give thanks to God the Father through him." Speech and action—that covers it.

In 1839, English author Edward Bulwer-Lytton said, "Beneath the rule of men entirely great / the pen is mightier than the sword."[11] In 1860, Abraham Lincoln said, "Actions speak louder than words."[12] Actions speak and words act. Christian practices are the speaking and doing of the gospel of God. The speech and action of the church comprise the practices of the church. The practices are the bread. We can hear, feel, taste, and see the practices of the congregation. The practices reveal, since the proof of the pudding is in the eating.

## Four Orienting Questions

Every individual Christian and each local congregation can increase its level of thoughtfulness regarding speech and action by allowing four orienting questions to probe their hearts and minds.

### *1. The Stewardship Question: Whose Am I?*

This question is the most basic and fundamental one that a Christian can ask. It also may be the most countercultural. The earliest Christians faced this ancient question that bears such contemporary significance. One of the earliest answers is found in 1 Corinthians 6:19-20: "Or don't you know that your body is a temple of the Holy Spirit who is in you? Don't you know that you have the Holy Spirit from God, and you don't belong to

---

11. Edward Bulwer-Lytton, *Richelieu: Or, the Conspiracy*, Act II, Scene 2, lines 307–308 (London: Saunders and Otley, 1839), 39.

12. Abraham Lincoln, "Cooper Union Address," lecture, New York, February 27, 1860, available online at https://www.abrahamlincolnonline.org/lincoln/speeches/cooper.htm.

yourselves? You have been bought and paid for so honor God with your body."

This answer is breathtaking and inspirational. "You don't belong to yourselves" breathes new life into our lives and is a major source of meaning and hope. The old Heidelberg Catechism called this our "comfort in life and death." It asked and answered the question this way:

> Question 1: What is your only comfort
> in life and in death?
>
> Answer: That I am not my own,
> but belong—
>
> body and soul,
> in life and in death—
>
> to my faithful Savior, Jesus Christ.[13]

The stewardship question helps guide our practices by calling us to see that our speech and action have a sacred source and fall under the judgment of the faithful Savior from whom the gifts of speech and power come. Christ is our life, and all our lives are his concern.

One of my (Matt's) most cherished pieces of art is so simple a child could have done it. The artist Stanley Miller, a member of FBC Waco and our friend, created it using grease pencil on a white page. It depicts a simple quote adorned with a treble clef. The quote reads, "O how he loves you and me." It is signed by Stanley Miller and Kurt Kaiser. Stanley gave this piece to me because he knows "O How He Loves You and Me" is my favorite song. I once preached a whole sermon series based on the little chorus. Mr. Kaiser came and played and sang for us. It was amazing.

Our family is moved to tears every time we sing "O How He Loves You and Me" because my uncle Steve Heblon chose it to be sung at his funeral. It was his witness. Uncle Steve died of leukemia when I was in elementary school. My mom's only sibling, Uncle Steve was larger than life to me. Our son bears his name. Steve was a young and popular schoolteacher. He knew his service would be packed with hurting kids, and he wanted the words of the song to declare the truth that defined his short life. The same words

13. Heidelberg Catechism, available online at https://www.crcna.org/welcome/beliefs/confessions/heidelberg-catechism.

defined Kurt Kaiser's long and fruitful life. They are the witness of every authentic follower of Christ: "He gave his life, what more could he give?"[14] That Christ gave his life in order to give us our lives is a basic theological truth with radical implications. We owe all to Christ. Our speech and actions are his concern for he is our life, as Colossians 3:4 declares.

Mr. Kaiser certainly understood this truth related to creativity and talents. He arranged thousands of songs and wrote just as many himself. His life was saturated with music but rooted in Christ. He once did an interview for the Laity Lodge Artist Series that spoke directly to his views about talent and God. His testimony gets to the heart of the stewardship question. He said, "My father early on taught me that whatever gift I'd been given, I should burnish it and shine it and make it as good as I could make it and then give it back to the one from whom I had received it."[15]

Belonging to Christ does not erase our uniqueness or humanity. It sanctifies it. Our lives come from the Lord and return to the Lord. Our gifts are from God's hand. We have the lifelong responsibility to burnish our gifts and give them back to God. No word or deed lacks meaning. They are either burnished gifts or tarnished gifts. "Whose am I?" We belong to Christ.

## 2. The Identity Question: Who Am I?

No two humans are exactly the same. Neither do any two churches have the exact same corporate personality. Our uniqueness reflects God's creativity and therefore must be honored.

We must pursue this orienting question with care because the ambient culture has coopted and twisted it in damaging ways. There is a saccharine theology today that gives lip service to original blessing without grappling with original sin. This version of our story is a creation *sans* fall view of life (and consequently *sans* redemption as well). We may call this "Lady Gaga theology." In this mindset, we can always be sure we are on the right track because we were "born this way," whatever way that happens to be.[16]

A young family in our congregation shared an illustrative story after a long car ride to Disney World. There is a ton of asphalt between Orlando,

---

14. Kurt Kaiser, "O How He Loves You and Me," Word Music, 1975.

15. Kurt Kaiser, "Using Your Gifts," video recording, Laity Lodge Foundation, October 5, 2012, available online at https://www.youtube.com/watch?v=5gE5g2B4Q9g.

16. Lady Gaga, "Born This Way," track 2 on *Born This Way*, 2011.

Florida, and Waco, Texas. They had three kids in a small SUV, the youngest in a car seat. Somewhere close to Biloxi, a fight broke out. The youngest declared to her older brother in acid tones, "I can't not hate you because God made me this way!" Ouch. Her parents were rightly concerned about her pint-sized heresy. Where did she get that idea? Might as well ask a fish where it found the water.

God made us. We have fallen short. God is redeeming us. This is the rhythm of Christian theology and the foundation stone for a faithful answer to the identity question. We are aspective yet whole. Different parts and features make up our lives. With these distinctives we can either honor or dishonor God. We can express our fallen identity or increasingly express God's redemptive grace. Understanding our unique identity in light of salvation is a core part of faithful Christian practice.

Saddleback Community Church pioneered the use of the S.H.A.P.E. schema to help Christians identify the unique way God formed them for life and ministry. The acronym stands for Spiritual Gifts, Heart, Abilities, Personality, and Experience.[17] S.H.A.P.E. assessments are widely available and can help individuals and churches explore the identity question. These aspects come together in our lives and determine the most impactful ways we are to speak and act in the world.

There is both continuity and discontinuity to our identity before and after God's saving grace touches our lives. As Christians we are created beings with an odd baptismal identity. Take the Apostle Paul as an example. Before his conversion, passion and zeal defined his life. Christ didn't douse that passion; he redirected it. Think also of Moses. His experiences in Egypt's palace and among Midian's flocks translated into his service to God and Israel. When we factor in all the ways God has shaped and continues to shape us for ministry, we may say with gratitude, "We're *reborn* this way."

### *3. The Supply Question: What Do I Have?*

The Lord has entrusted individual Christians and churches with assets. These assets help us decide what God would have us say and do in ministry. Luther Snow wisely observed, "Assets are easiest to see in a crisis."[18] When things get wild, we begin to notice how we can (re)invest in our communities

---

17. See Rick Warren, *The Purpose Driven Life* (Grand Rapids, MI: Zondervan, 2002), 234.

18. Luther K. Snow, *The Power of Asset Mapping: How Your Congregation Can Act on Its Gifts* (Herndon, VA: The Alban Institute, 2004), 8.

for the sake of the gospel. In the old television series *MacGyver*, week after week Richard Dean Anderson's character Angus "Mac" MacGyver would get out of a difficult situation using an odd assortment of assets. He put together things that didn't seem to go together to do what needed to be done.

*MacGyver* was entertaining because the creative use of assets is such a crucial part of life. One of the best illustrations of this reality is the "square peg in a round hole" scheme in the 1995 film *Apollo 13*. You'll want to rewatch this scene or experience it for the first time. A critical repair is needed to save the lives of American astronauts. An engineering supervisor in Houston, Texas, dumps a box full of stuff that is also onboard the Apollo module onto a table. The only assets at the engineers' (or astronauts'!) disposal are the ones they already have.

Those brilliant engineers made it work. This sequence wasn't film or television imagination. It was real life. One of those engineers is a member of University Baptist Church in Clear Lake, Texas. Retired NASA engineer Merlin Merritt reflects on his Apollo 13 experience and God's supply this way:

> For me, the flight of *Apollo 13* was not a failure but a flight of miracles. It was a flight protected by the Creator of life itself, who reached out in a miraculous way to provide a lifeboat for three astronauts whose lives literally hung in the balance of space. It was a miracle not unlike the one God performed for Noah and his family as recorded in the Bible, providing a safe environment for the crew and stretching life-supporting consumables as Jesus himself had miraculously stretched five loaves of bread and two fish to feed five thousand in the first century.[19]

The parable of the talents in Matthew 25:14-30 makes it clear that Jesus means for us to use the assets entrusted to us to serve his purposes in the world. We can be creative with how we use them knowing that the stuff piled in the box can be lifesaving and life-giving. Before God sent Moses to Egypt, God asked him, "What's that in your hand?" (Exod 4:2). Before Jesus fed a hungry multitude, he asked the disciples, "How much bread do you have?" (Mark 6:38). With a simple shepherd's staff, Moses bested the sorcerers of Pharaoh. With a boy's sack lunch, Jesus satisfied the hunger of a community. As we consider our Christian practices, we need to identify

19. W. Merlin Merritt, *Seeing the Son on the Way to the Moon: A NASA Engineer's Reflection on Science and Faith* (Macon, GA: Smyth & Helwys, 2018), 31–32.

our own "loaves and fishes." What has God placed in our hands? Sack lunches and shepherd's rods take on miraculous shape when we dedicate those assets to God.

### *4. The Service Question: What Shall I Do?*

Are you going to fish or cut bait? Practices are literally defined by saying and doing, by action. In his biography of Leonardo Da Vinci, Walter Isaacson makes the brilliant observation, "Vision without execution is hallucination."[20] We must be thoughtful about our practices, but eventually practices must be . . . well, practiced. We grow in ministry by doing ministry. We must ingest these orienting questions so that action takes on a more intuitive and reflective feel. When we speak and act in service to God and others, we can then reflect and grow from our experiences.

Louise Fletcher recently passed away at the age of eighty-eight. She was born in Birmingham, Alabama, to an Episcopal minister named Robert Fletcher and his wife Estelle, both of whom were deaf. When Louise received the Academy Award for her iconic role as Nurse Ratched in Ken Kesey's *One Flew Over the Cuckoo's Nest*, she received the award in American Sign Language as a tribute to her parents and their encouragement of her craft. Fletcher once reflected on her work saying, "The only way to be an actress is to act."[21] There is good guidance here. Vital Christianity is an activist faith.[22] We need to say, and we need to do. And all the doing and saying must be to the glory of God.

---

20. Walter Isaacson, *Leonardo Da Vinci* (New York: Simon and Schuster, 2017), 4.

21. Quoted by Nardine Saad, "Louise Fletcher, Oscar-winning actress who played Nurse Ratched in 'Cuckoo's Nest,' dies," *Los Angeles Times*, September 23, 2022, https://www.latimes.com/entertainment-arts/story/2022-09-23/louise-fletcher-dead-obit.

22. British Baptist historian David Bebbington identifies "activism" as one of four characteristics that define evangelicals, alongside conversionism, biblicism, and crucicentrism. See Bebbington, *Evangelicalism in Modern Britain: A History from the 1730s to the 1980s* (London: Routledge, 1989), 2–3. In Bebbington's usage, which we adopt here, activism is more than mere political mobilization. It refers instead to a holistic pattern of practice, a faith that works itself out through enacted daily expression for the good of the community.

## Me and We

One of the great tensions in life is the tension that arises between the individual and the collective. As Christians we have a personal relationship with God. Christ elevated and honored the individual. The faith of a single person in a crowd could touch him and arrest his attention (e.g., Mark 4:21-34). He also wept over whole cities and loved the crowd *as a crowd* (Luke 19:41-44). He gave his life for you *and* for his entire church. A powerful interplay exists between a lone disciple of Christ and the community of faith that Christ calls her to serve. How do these four orienting questions relate to the "me and we" nature of the Christian faith?

We need to embrace a twin responsibility. God has given us responsibility over our individual lives *and* the administration of local congregations. The church belongs to Christ. He is the head (Col 1:18). This makes sense because each individual believer belongs body and soul to him as well. Just as the individual must ask the orienting questions and speak and act by them, so must the churches.

John Smyth memorably expressed the conviction that the church must take responsibility for the church by calling for a "kingship of all believers." He said, "The Saynts as Kings . . . rule the visible church."[23] David Bebbington observes,

> This principle, the kingship of all believers, is perhaps Smyth's most enduring legacy. He accepted the general Reformation conviction of the priesthood of all believers, the status that gives access to the Father, but he added an entirely different point. Christians, he held, share in the kingly role of Christ as much as in his priestly role. Together they possess the authority of their ascended Lord to rule each local congregation. That, for Smyth, was the true foundation of church government.[24]

Theologians who have embraced versions of this "Baptist vision" include James McClendon, Jürgen Moltmann, and Miroslav Volf. Moltmann stated clearly that "the foundation of the church [is] the person of Christ, in his threefold messianic ministry and in his promised presence."[25] That

---

23. Quoted by David W. Bebbington, *Baptists through the Centuries: A History of a Global People*, 2nd ed. (Waco, TX: Baylor University Press, 2018), 33.

24. Bebbington, *Baptists*, 33.

25. Jürgen Moltmann, *The Church in the Power of the Spirit: A Contribution to Messianic Ecclesiology*, trans. Margaret Kohl (New York: Harper and Row, 1977), 133.

threefold ministry was and is prophet, priest, and king. Christians share these vocations by salvation and union with Christ. Shared congregational responsibility is the logical outcome.

This implication means we share equal responsibility before God for the faithful witness of the church. It does not, however, eliminate the need and value of leadership in the churches of Christ. Miroslav Volf built a vibrant congregational ecclesiology on the foundation of Smyth's vision. He affirms the need for leaders while maintaining universal responsibility by noting that leadership is a gift of the Holy Spirit. Volf writes,

> Universal distribution of the charismata implies *common responsibility* for the life of the church. Such common responsibility is compatible with the particular charismata of leadership ("office"). In the context of universal distribution of charismata, however, such leadership acquires a new profile. It cannot be the task of leaders, ordained or not, to do everything in the church themselves. That would lead to hypertrophy of this one member of the body of Christ and to a fateful atrophy of all other members. The task of leaders is first to animate all the members of the church to engage their pluriform charismatic activities, and then to coordinate these activities. Second, leaders are responsible for a mature church that is called to test every manifestation of the Spirit (see 1 Thess. 5:21).[26]

Every local church has leaders. These leaders must own the responsibility to help the body discern what the church is to say and do and to organize the practices of the church to mature the church and serve the community. This discernment and organization work best when the leadership of the church is diverse and mutually submitted to Christ and the congregation.[27] If you are reading this book, you are likely a leader in a local church. As you freshly commit to encourage Christian practices that emerge from a godly congregational culture and meet the needs of your ministry context, let us offer five final words of encouragement.

---

26. Miroslav Volf, *After Our Likeness: The Church as the Image of the Trinity* (Grand Rapids, MI: Eerdmans, 1998), 230 (emphasis original).

27. See David Fitch's work on the "Fivefold Gifting" (cf. Ephesians 4:11-13) in David E. Fitch, *Faithful Presence: Seven Disciplines that Shape the Church for Mission* (Downers Grove, IL: IVP Books, 2016), 149–66; and David E. Fitch, *Seven Practices for the Church on Mission* (Downers Grove, IL: IVP Books, 2018), 95–113.

### *1. Do what you know to do.*

God has given us so many clear directions on what we are to say and do in ministry that we could spend the rest of our lives without additional guidance. We know we are to worship and wait, play and pray. Many of us have also discerned a call to a particular action that is still left uncompleted. Colossians 4:17 is a fascinating verse. It says, "And tell Archippus, 'See to it that you complete the ministry that you received from the Lord.'" Archippus got called out in big church. Paul delivered a specific word of encouragement for him to start doing what the Lord had spoken to him about. One of the ways to discern which practices we should engage as a congregation is to look at what is left undone.

### *2. Ask the Lord.*

This one is so simple that it frequently evades us. Waiting on the Lord is not a passive reality. Earnest and sincere prayer permeates godly waiting. When we ask the Lord to clarify open doors and show us what to say and do, we need not be surprised when the Lord does just that.

### *3. Attend to open doors.*

The motif of an open door runs as a thread throughout the New Testament. God leads the church through open doors of opportunity. Challenges and opposition sometimes accompany these opportunities, but God works to place openings before us for meaningful life and work.

### *4. Act on desires and be open to correction.*

God often leads us though sanctified ambition, godly desire. Second Samuel 7 records a wonderful story. The chapter opens, "When the king was settled in his palace, and the LORD had given him rest from all his surrounding enemies, the king said to the prophet Nathan, 'Look! I'm living in a cedar palace, but God's chest is housed in a tent!' Nathan said to the king, 'Go ahead and do whatever you are thinking, because the LORD is with you'" (2 Sam 7:1-3). And the Lord was with David, but not in the way that he and Nathan initially thought. God would make it clear that the temple in David's mind was not his to build. That responsibility would fall to Solomon. God said it like this: "I will raise up your descendant—one of your very own children—to succeed you, and I will establish his kingdom. He will build a temple for my name, and I will establish his royal throne forever. I will be a father to him, and he will be a son to me" (2 Sam 7:12-14). Can you imagine how David received this word? God gave him something far better than he could have imagined. The Lord's NO gave way to a larger YES.

When we seek the kingdom of God above all else, we can stand on the promise of Christ's presence. He really is with us. We are therefore free to try, to act on the ideas in our minds and hearts. God loves us enough to send a few "nos" along the way as we live to find the "yeses."

## *5. Beware sins of omission.*

The best way for a leader to remain popular is to do relatively nothing. We often fear the risk associated with ministry action. Speaking and doing is risky, which leads to apprehension. We retreat to our heads and rest our feet. We need to accept that there is a tremendous risk that comes with inaction as well. The phrase we are looking for is "sins of omission." The memorable language of *The Book of Common Prayer* is instructive: "Most merciful God, we confess that we have sinned against you in thought, word, and deed, by what we have done, *and by what we have left undone*."[28] Make no mistake about it, the things we leave undone hurt us.

In his novel *Crusader's Cross*, James Lee Burke illustrates sins of omission with an arresting image: ". . . a sin of omission . . . can be like the rusty head of a hatchet buried in the heartwood of a tree—it eventually finds the teeth of a whirling saw blade."[29] Fellow Louisiana Catholic writer Tim Gautreaux dedicated an entire short story to the whirling saw-blade consequences of sins of omission. The story is titled "The Pine Oil Writers' Conference." The main character is a Presbyterian minister who dabbles in fiction writing. Coaxed into attending a writers' conference at a small community college, he finds it a rather disappointing experience because most of the participants are there merely to avoid their lives and imbibe the mystique of being writers. The heart of the story emerges when a conference leader named Faye Cooker interrogates the pastor. Faye appreciates

---

28. The Episcopal Church, *The Book of Common Prayer* (New York: Oxford University Press, 2007), 360 (emphasis added).

29. James Lee Burke, *Crusader's Cross* (New York: Simon and Schuster, 2005), 22. Burke reflects on the likely inspiration for this image from his own childhood in "James Lee Burke's Bayou Baptism," *Garden & Gun*, December 2022, available at https://gardenandgun.com/articles/james-lee-burkes-bayou-baptism/.

his talents and wants him to go all in to develop them. Their conversation goes like this:

> "Why do you want to write, anyway?"
> "I want to find out if I can do it well, if it's what I do best."
> "And then what?"
> "Then it'll be as though I have a good voice. I guess I should sing."
> "A sense of duty to your talent," she mused, looking up at a dusty vinyl plant hanging from the ceiling. "My old preacher used to talk about that. . . . He said that those who could do good work but wouldn't created a vacuum in the world that would be filled by those who could do bad things and would."[30]

The rest of the story is a testimony to the truth of the old preacher's observation. When we do what God calls us to do, when we are faithful and consistent, we are part of repairing *shalom* in a broken world.

The ongoing and occasional practices of the church are how the world knows us and comes to know our Christ. All the ingredients of congregational culture work together to create words and deeds that are life-giving for all who partake of them. Words of witness and deeds of love flow from Christ-honoring beliefs, attitudes, values, and goals. May we work the dough of congregational soul culture. May the Holy Spirit's fire bake the loaves. May the hungry partake. May we all declare, "Taste and see how good the LORD is! The one who takes refuge in him is truly happy!" (Ps 34:8).

---

30. Tim Gautreaux, "The Pine Oil Writers' Conference," in *Welding with Children* (New York: Picador, 1999), 112.

Chapter 6

# Practices

## Questions for Further Reflection

1. Read through Colossians 3 and then Galatians 5 and record a list of the attitudes that Paul prescribes for Christians in each passage. Then, highlight or circle the attitudes that you find in *both* passages.

| Colossians 3 | Galatians 5 |
|---|---|
| | |

2. Read C. S. Lewis's short essay "The Inner Ring" (available at https://www.lewissociety.org/innerring/). The passion to belong to "the inner ring" usually arises from greed or fear. Which one tempts you most?

_______________

_______________

_______________

_______________

_______________

3. Cormac McCarthy warns how the two emotions of greed and fear make "smart people do dumb things" because they've embraced "a set of beliefs . . . at odds with reality."[I] Spend a few minutes in prayer confessing your own greed and fear. Ask the Lord to give you a clear understanding of reality so that you can live and serve with wisdom in the world.

4. Walker Percy wrote, "Lucky is the man who does not secretly believe that every possibility is open to him."[II] How do you respond? Do you tend to see limits as a gift or as a hindrance? What are some of the limits that the Lord has given to you?

_______________

_______________

_______________

_______________

_______________

5. What are some elements of your S.H.A.P.E.?

1) Spiritual Gifts (see 1 Corinthians 12; Romans 12; Ephesians 4; etc.):

_______________

_______________

_______________

2) Heart (passions and animating concerns):

_______________

_______________

_______________

I. Cormac McCarthy, *The Passenger* (New York: Knopf, 2022), 269.
II. Walker Percy, *The Last Gentleman* (New York: Picador, 1966), 4.

3) Abilities (particular skills and talents):

________________________________________

________________________________________

________________________________________

4) Personality:

________________________________________

________________________________________

________________________________________

5) Experiences:

________________________________________

________________________________________

________________________________________

6. Are you guilty of any sins of omission? What things have you "left undone"? Spend 5–10 minutes in prayer confessing these things to Christ and seeking restoration.

# Chapter 6: Practices

## *Group Discussion Guide*

1. Many Christian practices occur on a regular rhythm. What are your church's practices . . .

- Daily (you might rely on personal practices of church members here, or maybe not)?
- Weekly?
- Yearly?

2. Are there any church practices that are repeated but more occasional?

3. Divide into small groups and share stories about someone who became great by first deciding to be good (like Red Covington in our chapter). After 10–15 minutes, have each group share one reflection with the entire group.

4. Return to your small groups and have each participant discuss what "psalms, hymns, and spiritual songs" (Col 3:16) have shaped their beliefs the most. What songs do you hope to sing in your final weeks? What song would you like sung at your memorial?

5. Spend a few minutes in prayer thanking the Lord for those who gave these songs to the church and for others who gave them to you personally. Then, reconvene and list some favorites.

6. What is *the* song of your church? If your church adopted a congregational anthem, what would it be and why? *(List responses and capture them for later. You might vote or otherwise select a "winner," or you might simply compile a list of "nominees.")*

7. Watch Kurt Kaiser's interview with Laity Lodge (approximately 7 minutes, available at https://www.youtube.com/watch?v=5gE5g2B4Q9g).

- What gifts has the Lord given to you? *(Invite responses from the group.)*
- How can you "burnish and shine them" to present back to the Lord?

Next, read Isaiah 66:18-23 aloud together. In this remarkable passage, the Lord gathers "all nations and cultures" in their contrasting diversity to "declare [the Lord's] glory among the nations" (vv. 18-19). The Lord promises to select some to serve as "priests and Levites" (v. 21), an astonishing promise from the Old Testament of God's intention to use the Gentiles (most of us!) with their distinct gifts not only as worshipers but even as worship leaders.

8. Crises tend to reveal and clarify assets.

- What crises has your congregation weathered together?
- What assets did they reveal?
- "What's that in your hand?" (Exodus 4:2)
- "How much bread do you have?" (Mark 6:38)
- Did you continue to employ these assets in service to the Lord after the crisis had passed?

9. How do you respond to the idea of "the kingship of all believers"? How do we reign in partnership with one another? Is there a tension between this radically egalitarian vision and God's gifting and call of leaders to serve the church? *(Discuss in small groups.)*

10. Miroslav Volf warns of danger when leaders "do everything in the church themselves,"[31] and the "80/20 Rule" (the idea that 80 percent of the work is done by 20 percent of the people) has become a cliché in church life.

- Who are the leaders in your church? Think in terms not only of positional authority but also, and maybe especially, of practical service.
- How much of the load do these leaders carry? In other words, how much of the *doing* do they *do*? Is there genuine sharing of responsibility and service across the congregation?

11. What does your church *already know* to do? Are you doing it?

---

31. Miroslav Volf, *After Our Likeness: The Church as the Image of the Trinity* (Grand Rapids, MI: Eerdmans, 1998), 230.

# 7. Soulful Leadership in a World of Calendars and Covenants

*So now, be strong, Zerubbabel, says the* Lord. *Be strong, High Priest Joshua, Jehozadak's son, and be strong, all you people of the land, says the* Lord. *Work, for I am with you, says the* Lord *of heavenly forces. As with our agreement when you came out of Egypt, my spirit stands in your midst. Don't fear.*

**Haggai 2:4-5**

"When Harold Macmillan became Britain's prime minister, he was asked what would determine his government's course. He replied with Edwardian languor: 'Events, dear boy, events.'"[1] George Will wrote those words in a piece aptly titled "Events, Dear Boy, Events." He would go on to say in the column, "Pesky things, events. As usual, they are in the saddle, riding mankind."[2] That is a powerful image, isn't it? Events, sitting in the saddle, whip in hand, shining spurs digging into our sides—riding us.

I think we all agree with Mr. Will that events are powerful. But can we go as far as he does and place events on the back of the horse, riding humankind? That notion is the fruit of the immanent frame, the closed, godless world.[3]

---

1. George F. Will, "'Events, Dear Boy, Events,'" *Newsweek*, January 27, 2002, https://www.newsweek.com/events-dear-boy-events-143481.

2. Ibid.

3. See Charles Taylor, *A Secular Age* (Cambridge, MA: Belknap, 2007).

George Will once described himself as "an amiable, low-voltage atheist" that is married to "a fierce Presbyterian."[4] Imagine what that marriage must be like from time to time! I can see the Wills sitting together in the morning, talking over eggs and toast. Perhaps on the bright morning in 2002 when he wrote those pesky words about pesky events, Mrs. Will pushed back the way that fierce Presbyterians sometimes do. Maybe she said, "Oh honey, events are powerful, but they don't hold the reins; they aren't sovereign. Events, dear boy, don't get the last word."

We live in a world of clocks and calendars. They are among the chief tools we use to mark life, to chart history. As followers of Christ, we confess that this can't be the only way we think about the world and its history. G. Ernest Wright once said, "[H]istory [is] the arena of God's activity."[5] History, marked by its clocks and calendars, is touched by "the gracious hand of . . . God." This phrase found in Ezra 7:9 is taken from the secular court. It testifies to divine action in the world. Paul used a similar phrase in Philippians 1:18-19 when he said, "Yes, and I will continue to rejoice, for I know that through your prayers and the help [supply] of the Spirit of Jesus Christ this will turn out for my deliverance" (NRSV). They used calendars in Babylon and Rome to mark events, but these events weren't superior to the supply of the Spirit. The God of covenants works in the clock-and-calendar world to deliver and save. We must keep this truth before us as we think together about leadership.

Will Willimon said, "Leadership is necessary only if an organization needs to go somewhere and if an organization is accountable to a mission more important than its own survival."[6] That description fits every Christian church. We are accountable to Jesus and his overwhelmingly important goal of seeking the kingdom of God. We are heading somewhere. In the words of the old hymn, "We're marching to Zion."[7] Since this is true for us, we need leadership of a particular kind. We need the kind of spiritual,

---

4. Nicholas G. Hahn III, "George Will: The RealClearReligion Interview," *RealClearReligion*, September 22, 2014, https://www.realclearreligion.org/articles/2014/09/22/george_will_the_realclearreligion_interview.html.

5. G. Ernest Wright, *God Who Acts: Biblical Theology as Recital*, Studies in Biblical Theology 8 (London: SCM Press, 1952), 38.

6. William H. Willimon, *Leading with the Sermon: Preaching as Leadership* (Minneapolis: Fortress Press, 2020), 31.

7. Isaac Watts, "Come, We That Love the Lord," 1707, no. 549 in *Celebrating Grace Hymnal* (Macon, GA: Celebrating Grace, 2010).

soulful leadership that *looks* at clocks and calendars but *lives* by covenant with God, one that both plans and prays.

The book of Ezra is a great case study of soulful leadership. The people of God definitely needed to get somewhere, and they were certainly accountable to a mission more important than their own survival. A powerful event had marked the Jews of the books of Ezra and Nehemiah. The exile had profoundly shaped Israel. This season of history so defined those who endured it that they were sometimes simply called the exiles.

The Jews of the exilic period watched waves of events sweep over them. The temple in Jerusalem suffered at the hands of Babylon in 597 BC. The Babylonians removed temple treasures and began to deport people. In 586 BC they destroyed the temple itself.

The Babylonians settled deported Jews throughout their empire to supply labor. Life for many Jewish exiles was relatively prosperous. They worked in agriculture, commerce, and administration. During the captivity, Aramaic became the principal language of the Jewish people. The Babylonians allowed the exiles a measure of autonomy. This freedom included latitude to practice their religion.

During the exile the prophecies of Jeremiah and Ezekiel shaped the captives in rich ways. Before the fall of Jerusalem, many had ignored the messages of God's prophets. Their predictions of the fall of the city and the razing of the temple seemed overly alarmist . . . until those things happened. Jeremiah had looked like a total failure during his lifetime. Sometimes a message from God has a long fuse. Both Ezekiel and Jeremiah mingled strong words of judgment with stronger words of continued purpose and hope. They spoke of a return from captivity. Their prophecies would nourish the faith of the Jews in the meantime. Jeremiah's messages became one of the main reasons for the survival of the Jewish faith during the exile. Covenant would invade calendars.

Cyrus II, the leader of the Persian dynasty, conquered Babylon in 538 BC. He quickly instituted new policies. He issued a decree that the exiled Jews could return to Jerusalem to rebuild the city and reestablish worship in the temple. The Jews interpreted this decree as the gracious hand of God in history, the Supply of the Spirit, if you will. Ezra 1:1 reads, "In the first year of King Cyrus of Persia's rule, to fulfill the LORD's word spoken to Jeremiah, the LORD stirred up the spirit of Persia's King Cyrus . . . ." Ezra-Nehemiah's episodic narratives offer stories that further illustrate God's stirring grace during challenge, victory, disappointment, discouragement, sin, and resilient hope. It is a primer on soulful leadership.[8]

Episode 1 comes in Ezra 1–2 and illustrates God's providence. As we've noted, Ezra 1:1 opens the book with a strong note of providence. God was acting on God's word in the world. Grace met the exilic judgment. God's hand would touch the people, and *promptings* would mark God's spiritual supply. Ezra 1:5a asserts that the same God who stirred the heart of Cyrus stirred the heart of the Jews. The idea of promptings reminds us that we do not dwell in a closed universe. God is God, and God prompts.

God's promptings led to *preparation.* Ezra 1:5b notes that the people began to prepare for the return to Jerusalem to reestablish temple worship. Spiritual renewal needs organized religion. For organized religion to avoid becoming lifeless and rote, soulful leadership is essential.

Soulful leadership is also vital because *pluriformity* marks God's work. Ezra 1:6 says that some of the Jews moved to Jerusalem, but *all* were part of the movement to restore worship in Jerusalem. Not every person did the same thing in response to the open door from God. Unity does not require uniformity.

The second episode is found in Ezra 3–6 and the book of Haggai. The remnant returned and began to work under Zerubbabel. The project would prove to be a roller coaster ride that took decades to complete. Recall that opposition often accompanies open doors from God. Both highs and lows would mark the job. Only God's word and soulful leadership would bring them through. Episode 2 includes several distinct movements. The first one is *praise.* In Ezra 3:10-11, God's people celebrated the rebuilding of the altar. They passionately thanked God for getting them to a crucial milestone. Gratitude and thanksgiving are vital practices that should be present in every congregation.

Unfortunately, the note of praise proved short-lived. *Pain* also marked the episode. In Ezra 3:12–4:5, the exiles experienced the pain of disappointment and discouragement. The disappointment came from the size of the temple's rebuilt foundations in comparison to the Solomonic temple. The ancients wept with disappointment when they saw the construction. Those already living in the land also actively discouraged the Jews when they returned. Open doors and opposition are like peas and carrots.

---

8. Portions of this chapter originally appeared in Matt Snowden, "I'll Be There with Bells On: 7 Marks of Priestly Pastoral Ministry from the Book of Ezra," *Preaching Today*, https://www.preachingtoday.com/exegesis/ezra/ill-be-there-with-bells-on.html.

Discouragement and disappointment led to a common congregational disease: *paralysis*. The work came to a full stop. The people turned their attention to piddling around. They lost the mission entirely. How many congregations are in a state of soul paralysis? In this state there is plenty of piddly activity but little to no action toward the fulfillment of the call of God. Busyness supplants kingdom-building.

The saving grace for the Jews was the soulful leadership that came from the prophets Haggai and Zechariah and the arrival of Ezra himself. Ezra 5:1-2 reads, "Then the prophet Haggai and the prophet Zechariah, Iddo's son, prophesied to the Jews who were in Judah and Jerusalem in the name of Israel's God who was over them. Subsequently, Zerubbabel, Shealtiel's son, and Jeshua, Jozadak's son, began to rebuild God's house in Jerusalem. God's prophets were with them, helping them." The prophets of God helped the paralyzed people. The book of Ezra continues to say in 6:14 that the Jews "built and prospered because of the prophesying . . . ."

The church needs prophetic help. Recall our earlier discussion of the prophethood of all believers. We are to be a people who speak the Spirit-animated word of God to each other. Roger Stronstad said of this dynamic, "the theophany at Mt Sinai established Israel as a kingdom of priests, the theophany on the day of Pentecost establishes the disciples as a community of prophets."[9] The word of God breaks through the discouragement and disappointment and reenergizes the work of God.

Soulful leadership unites word and Spirit. The prophets welded these two gifts, and so did Ezra. Ezra joined the Jews in Jerusalem and modeled life-giving ministry. Ezra 7:10 is one of the finest summaries of faithful ministry in the Bible: "Ezra had determined to study and perform the LORD's instruction, and to teach law and justice in Israel." The description of the good parson in *Canterbury Tales* fits Ezra and every truly soulful Christian leader: "He was a model his flock could understand, for first he did and afterward he taught."[10] Soulful leadership is a matter of show and tell. It is help and word.

Few places in all of Scripture chronicle the processes of soulful leadership better than Ezra 8:15-23. It records the fourth full episode in Ezra-Nehemiah, and it tells the story of how Ezra left Babylon for Jerusalem

---

9. Roger Stronstad, *The Prophethood of All Believers: A Study in Luke's Charismatic Theology* (Cleveland, TN: CPT Press, 2010), 53.

10. Geoffrey Chaucer, *The Canterbury Tales*, in *The Portable Chaucer*, rev. ed., ed. and trans. Theodore Morrison (New York: Penguin, 1977), 66.

leading a group that would help rebuild the temple. The story shows how godly, soulful leadership kindles hope. In this story we discern a process of leadership marked by purposeful acts of soulful leaders. We will spend the rest of this chapter carefully exploring this process.

## Four Processes of Soulful Leadership

### *Convening*

Soulful leaders *convene*. Ezra 8:15 reads, "I gathered them by the river that runs to Ahava, and there we camped for three days." "I gathered them" implies power, a good power. Ezra revealed that he had convening power. To convene is to bring people and assets together. On a little canal in Babylon, Ezra called a meeting and got things moving. If congregations and institutions are healthy and vibrant, then soulful leaders are using convening power.

I (Matt) was once in a meeting with my friend Dennis Wiles, pastor of the First Baptist Church of Arlington, Texas. During the meeting he mentioned a legendary Arlington pastor named N. L. Robinson. Pastor Robinson led the Mount Olive Missionary Baptist Church for over fifty years. Dennis said, "Pastor Robinson just had convening power. When he called you showed up." I was fascinated by that turn of phrase and pressed Dennis about it. He said he borrowed the idea from sociologist and university president Michael Lindsay. Lindsay describes convening power in his book *View from the Top: An Inside Look at How People in Power See and Shape the World.*[11] It is simply the ability to bring people together and get things done.

We believe that there are a least three types of convening power, and all are necessary aspects of soulful leadership. The first type is *positional* convening power. Groups confer this power through official action. This authority comes with holding office. Hugh Heclo's insights are helpful:

> The term "office" comes down to us from the Latin, mainly by way of the Roman classics and church history. Compounded from the words for "work" and "to do," *officium* indicates the performance of a task, with heavy overtones of a duty to perform properly. . . . With the rise of Christianity and the organized church, *officium* took on added meaning. It meant being charged with special duty and trust of a more sacred nature,

---

11. D. Michael Lindsay, *View from the Top: An Inside Look at How People in Power See and Shape the World* (Hoboken, NJ: Wiley, 2014).

> as in Paul, "an apostle to the gentiles," magnifying his "office" (Romans 11:13).[12]

Every church has officers. They wear different titles, but make no mistake, every congregation has them. We need to cultivate an attitude of sacred duty to convene the people for a mission greater than our own institutional survival.

The second type of convening power is *practical*. It is an unofficial authority born of respect and influence. A person with practical convening power can gather the people with or without holding some recognized office. This authority may emerge from the leadership charism. Some folks have a romantic view of common church life. They embrace a shallow version of egalitarianism in which leadership is radically flat. Governance is by consensus, sitting in a circle. Have you been around that table? It begins with waiting. Waiting for what? For the person with convening power to gather it up and get it started. We can't escape the need for soulful leadership. Every healthy congregation has unofficial leaders who sometimes also hold office. Through the strength of their lives, they call us together.

The third type of convening power is the power to gather all the aspects of your personal life into a single whole. We can call this *personal* convening power. Integrity is the fruit of personal conveying power, and it is the basis for all life-giving soulful leadership. Instability in the congregation and organization is the fruit of personal instability. James 1:8 states clearly, "a double-minded man [is] unstable in all his ways" (ESV). Michael Lindsay says that "people in power, if they succeed for any length of time, lead not through their roles or their authority. Instead, they lead with their lives."[13] Ezra led through his life. Shaping congregational soul culture for the mission of God will require soulful leaders marked by integrity using convening power for God's glory and the good of people.

## Coordinating

Soulful leaders *coordinate*. Ezra convened the people on the banks of the Ahava in the beginning of 8:15. The second part of the verse reads, "As I reviewed the people and the priests, I found no Levites there." Reviewing the people and priests was an act of coordinating power. In his book

12. Hugh Heclo, *On Thinking Institutionally* (Oxford: Oxford University Press, 2008), 136–37.

13. Lindsay, *View from the Top*, xviii.

*Leadership Is an Art*, Max De Pree famously said, "The first responsibility of a leader is to define reality. The last is to say thank you. In between the two, the leader must become a servant and a debtor."[14] Defining reality is the outgrowth of coordinating power.

Have you ever been on a long bus trip with a big group of people? Every missionary, marching band, basketball team, youth ministry, senior adult, or bird-watching bus trip starts the same way: participants show up early or fashionably late. Some bring enough luggage to circumnavigate the globe, while at least one packs in a plastic bag from Walgreens. Folks loiter in the parking lot, chat, flirt, complain, and wait. What are they waiting on? They are waiting on the review. The leaders are checking a list. Do we have everyone? Everything? Are we ready to go? Coordinating power isn't a superpower, but it is a needed one.

Ezra reviewed the camp for three full days. He was acting as overseer. An overseer must do two things in order to define reality: first, understand the situation and, then, clearly communicate it to the community.

If we want to coordinate well, we must develop the ability to pay attention. Simone Weil was a brilliant person. At the age of ten, she announced that she had become a Communist. She later realized that she'd never met a Communist, so when Trotsky came to Paris, she went out to see him. When she observed him, she made an odd discovery. He seemed to have an affection for "humanity" but didn't seem to care for actual people. This experience would set her on a different course. She would eventually latch on to the biblical story of the Good Samaritan (Luke 10:25-37). "Seeing" is at the heart of Jesus's parable; the priest, Levite, and Samaritan each "saw" the victimized man beside the road (Luke 10:31-33), but they had radically different responses.

Weil began to think deeply about an optics of hope. She would eventually write an essay for Catholic students titled "Reflections on the Right Use of School Studies with a View to the Love of God."[15] With stunning insight, she said, "Not only does the love of God have attention for its substance; the love of our neighbor, which we know to be the same love, is made of this same substance."[16] Paying attention is the substance of love.

---

14. Max De Pree, *Leadership Is an Art* (New York: Currency, 2004), 11.

15. Simone Weil, "Reflections on the Right Use of School Studies with a View to the Love of God," in *Waiting for God*, trans. Emma Craufurd (New York: Harper and Row, 1951), 105–16.

16. Ibid., 114.

The film *Lady Bird* beautifully illustrates this idea.[17] This motion picture is a coming-of-age story about a young woman named Lady Bird. In one scene Lady Bird meets with a school nun named Sister Sarah Joan. Sister Sarah Joan is advising Lady Bird on her college admissions. The content of her essay comes up, and the conversation goes like this:

"You clearly love Sacramento," Sister Sarah Joan tells her.

Lady Bird, surprised, says, "I do?"

"You write about Sacramento so affectionately," the nun says, "and with such care."

"Well," Lady Bird replies, "I was just describing it."

"Well, it comes across as love," Sister Sarah Joan says.

"Sure," Lady Bird says unconvincingly. "I guess I pay attention."

Sister Sarah Joan then makes her point in the form of a question: "Don't you think maybe they are the same thing—love and attention?"

Love motivates coordinating power. Paying careful attention is what love does. Ezra took necessary time to review the community of faith, and he serves as a role model for us as we work the ingredients of vibrant congregational soul culture.

Coordinating is not just paying attention. It is also understanding the current situation and being able to communicate it clearly to the people. After completing his three-day review, Ezra plainly said, "I found no Levites there." This was a problem. Ezra modeled the old preacher advice, "Just tell the truth and trust the people." Difficult challenges often arise in ministry because ministry is life. Some leaders force-feed saccharine ideas to people to avoid hard things. We should simply opt out of that. It puts us at odds with reality. Prison warden and Mississippi Corrections Commissioner Burl Cain often says, "Nothing stays fixed."[18] Responding to shortfalls and needs is a part of coordinating ministry. Clear communication is a top-tier leadership art.

## *Collaborating*

Soulful leaders *collaborate*. To collaborate is to work together. Congregations and institutions often do not possess all the elements needed for success. Thinking back on our NASA engineers and the Apollo 13 challenges, we

---

17. *Lady Bird*, directed by Greta Gerwig, 2017, Universal Pictures.

18. Personal communication with the author, 2015. See Michael Hallett et al., *The Angola Prison Seminary: Effects of Faith-Based Ministry on Identity Transformation, Desistance, and Rehabilitation* (New York: Routledge, 2016).

must acknowledge that sometimes the needed fix isn't found inside the box. When this is the case, God often provides from outside the box. The skill of collaboration is needed to lead congregations and organizations into successful engagements. This was certainly the case in Ezra 8. When no Levites were found camping on the Ahava Canal, the mission wasn't over. Ezra led the people to collaborate with the people of Casiphia to provide Levites for the mission. Ezra 8:16-20 records it this way:

> I found no Levites there. So, I called Eliezer, Ariel, Shemaiah, Elnathan, Jarib, Elnathan, Nathan, Zechariah, and Meshullam, all leaders, together with Joiarib and Elnathan, who were wise. I sent them to Iddo, the leader at the place named Casiphia, telling them what to say to Iddo and his colleagues the temple servants at Casiphia, namely, to send us ministers for God's house. Because we were favored of God, they brought us Sherebiah, a skillful man of the house of Mahli, Levi's son and Israel's grandson, together with his sons and relatives so that there were eighteen in total. They also brought us Hashabiah and with him Jeshaiah of the family of Merari, together with his relatives and their sons so that there were twenty in total. In addition, there were two hundred twenty temple servants whom David and the princes had appointed to serve the Levites. They were all recorded by name.

This is the type of text we read rapidly during our one-year read-through-the-Bible plans. It deserves a closer look because it illustrates God's favor and the need to collaborate. Sometimes the answers to our challenges require working with others. We must collaborate with care in order to avoid malforming the mission.

We recently sat down over biscuits with physician John Anderson and healthcare executive Joel Allison to discuss organizational leadership. John and Joel are both deacons at First Baptist Church Waco and spent their careers in healthcare, many of them leading together at Baylor Health Care System (BHCS). John is a surgeon and was the Senior Vice President for Clinical Integration. Joel was CEO. They led together through some major transitions at BHCS. They worked to improve six domains of ideal patient care. John coined the acronym STEEEP to describe their areas of concern: safety, timeliness, effectiveness, efficiency, equity, and patient centeredness.[19]

---

19. See David J. Ballard, ed., *Achieving STEEEP Health Care* (Boca Raton, FL: CRC Press, 2014).

While they were pursuing improvement in these domains, the hospital system also had to discern opportunities for mergers, collaborations, and other organizational changes. How did they go about all this transformation? The striking thing about Joel and John was how often they referred to Baylor Hospital's founding statement. They both knew it by heart and used it to analyze decisions. When George W. Truett passionately advocated for building a Baptist hospital in Dallas in the early 1900s, he said, "Is it not now time to begin the erection of a great humanitarian hospital, one to which men of all creeds or those of none may come with equal confidence?"[20] This founding statement shaped both innovation and collaboration. Ezra's collaboration built capacity for the mission, but it didn't change the mission itself. The same was true for John and Joel at Baylor.

Collaboration and innovation grow from deep roots. Hugh Heclo said it this way: "Innovation is not meant to change the game. Legitimate innovation is meant to realize, with greater skill and fidelity, the larger potential of what the game is. In a line from Goethe that the late Jaroslav Pelikan liked to quote, 'What you have received as heritage, take now as task and thus you will make it your own.'"[21] John and Joel received a heritage and took it as their task. Ezra did so as well. So did the leaders from Casiphia. By retrieving their original calling and identity, they were able to collaborate for an expanded work in the world.

## Consecrating

Soulful leaders *consecrate*. Soulful Christian leadership is unique. It is rooted in the core conviction that the work is the Lord's and that we are invited to join in it. Soulful leaders humbly ask God for supernatural provision, give thanks for what God provides, and plainly discard the notions that we are in charge or control of any of it.

Ezra called for a fast in 8:21 to seek help from God. The text says, "Then I called for a fast there at the Ahava River so that we might submit before our God and ask of him a safe journey for ourselves, our children, and all our possessions." Prayer should not be a perfunctory item for ministry leaders. The apostle Paul often asked his sisters and brothers in the faith to pray for him even as he committed to pray for them. One of the best ways

---

20. Quoted by A. E. McGill, "The City and the Hospital: Why Dallas Rallied," *D Magazine*, August 1, 1997, https://www.dmagazine.com/publications/d-magazine/1997/august/the-city-the-hospital-why-dallas-rallied/.

21. Heclo, *On Thinking Institutionally*, 99.

to begin a season of renewal in a congregation is to organize a strategic prayer ministry.

God was faithful, and so were the people. They set out and journeyed to Jerusalem. What they did upon arrival is instructive for us. Ezra 8:32 says, "After arriving in Jerusalem, we rested there three days." They began in prayer, engaged the work, and then rested. Rest is as spiritual as work and prayer. It builds spiritual and emotional health and serves as a witness to God's "Godness." Many important works have derailed because leaders forgot to rest.

Peter Scazzero warns, "Emotionally unhealthy leaders do not practice Sabbath."[22] They confuse serving God with being God and conflate God's kingdom with our own. Some leaders behave this way all the time, and all leaders are probably guilty of this temptation some of the time.

Walker Percy offered a sobering warning in his novel *The Second Coming*. The narrator confesses, "I made straight A's and flunked ordinary living."[23] It is a shameful scandal that ministry sometimes replaces God in a person's life. "Success," personally defined, becomes the end. We must be intentional to avoid this trap. Paul seemed to have this purpose in mind in 1 Corinthians 9:26-27: "So now this is how I run—not without a clear goal in sight. I fight like a boxer in the ring, not like someone who is shadowboxing. Rather, I'm landing punches on my own body and subduing it like a slave. I do this to be sure that I myself won't be disqualified after preaching to others." The aim not to be disqualified is sobering. It clears our vision and chastens our drives. Consecrating our ministry through prayer and rest is a grace God gives us to keep us moving forward in a godly way.

Ambition is not wrong. Ambition born of greed or fear, however, is toxic. R. T. Kendall recently received an award for a lifetime of faithful ministry at Truett Seminary's National Preaching Conference. We hosted this conference at FBC Waco and witnessed Dr. Kendall receive the award with grace and a bit of embarrassment. He went on to preach a message about the anointing. He defines the anointing as "a gift that functions easily when it's working."[24] It is how God shapes us for service. Accepting our

---

22. Peter Scazzero, *The Emotionally Healthy Leader: How Transforming Your Inner Life Will Deeply Transform Your Church, Team, and World* (Grand Rapids, MI: Zondervan, 2015), 32.

23. Walker Percy, *The Second Coming* (New York: Picador, 1980), 93.

24. R. T. Kendall, *The Anointing: Yesterday, Today, Tomorrow* (Nashville: Thomas Nelson, 1999), 4.

anointing is part of consecrating the work of God. This focuses our ambition. Kendall says,

> The question is, will we accept our anointing? Or will we let ambition and personal drive for recognition get in the way? Martin Luther said that God uses sex to drive a person to marriage, ambition to drive a person to service, and fear to drive a person to faith. But if the *eros* love that may have a lot to do with making a couple want to get married is not paralleled by *agape* love (selfless concern), that marriage will eventually be on the rocks. Likewise, if ambition is not paralleled by a love for the honor of God, we will make the grievous mistake of moving outside our own anointing. This is partly why Jesus asked the question "How can you believe if you accept praise from one another, yet make no effort to obtain the praise that comes from the only God?" (John 5:44).

We can succeed in "ministry" and flunk life.

The only way to avoid this failure is to consecrate the work of God. We ask for God's blessing and power, and we practice sabbath. Resting on a sabbath is a regular reminder that God is God. When the Lord delivered Israel from Egyptian slavery, they were given the gift of sabbath to remind them that they were neither commodities nor compassionless masters. They were human beings in service to a living God. Hear the good word of Moses: "Do your work in six days. But on the seventh day you should rest so that your ox and donkey may rest, and even the child of your female slave and the immigrant may be refreshed. Be careful to obey everything that I have said to you. Don't call on the names of other gods. Don't even mention them" (Exod 23:12-13). Old Testament scholar Walter Brueggemann comments on this command with pastoral wisdom and precision: "The 'other gods' are agents and occasions of anxiety. But we, by discipline, by resolve, by baptism, by Eucharist, and by passion, resist such seductions. In so doing we stand alongside the creator in whose image we are made. By the end of six days God had done all that was necessary for creation . . . so have we!"[25]

Agents and occasions of anxiety abound. Church life is not immune to them—congregational life is a prime arena for the arrows of anxiety. The American mantra, "If it's going to be, it's up to me," can take over a congregational culture. Out of fear and greed, we'll try just about anything. To be

25. Walter Brueggemann, *Sabbath as Resistance: Saying No to the Culture of Now* (Louisville, KY: Westminster John Knox, 2014), 33.

"realistic" we become at odds with reality. God is the most real reality. God is God. God's work done God's way will never lack God's supply. When we consecrate the work through prayer and rest, we develop a "God is God" mindset. A simpler word for this mindset is *faith*. "It's impossible to please God without faith" (Heb 11:6). With faith mountains can move (see Matt 17:20).

Leadership is not necessary if we do not serve a mission larger than ourselves or do not want to go anywhere. If we profess to follow Christ, we profess the larger mission and journey of God. We profess our need for leadership. Soulful leadership is by the book, the Good Book. The biblical example of Ezra provides a helpful model for us as we follow God and lead God's church. In honor of God and for the love of God's people, we can convene, coordinate, collaborate, and consecrate the work to which God has called us.

Chapter 7

# Soulful Leadership in a World of Calendars and Covenants

## Questions for Further Reflection

1. The chapter began with former Prime Minister Macmillan's assertion that events would shape his government. What are the key events that have formed you and shaped your life, ministry, and leadership? Draw them as a timeline below.

2. At what points in your life do you recognize God intervening, redirecting the course of mere events?

3. Read through the book of Ezra, preferably in a single sitting (about half an hour). In the chart below, record the *calendar events* that happened to the returning Jewish exiles and the *covenant intervention* of the Lord on their behalf.

| Calendar Events | Covenant Intervention |
|---|---|
| | |

4. When has God "stirred up" your heart, as God did among the Jewish leaders in Ezra 1:5?

5. Ezra both taught and demonstrated faithfulness as he "[studied] and [performed] the Lord's instruction" (Ezra 7:10). What leaders in your life have welded instruction and practice in their ministries? Pause to thank God for them, and if you're able, thank them also!

   (1)

   (2)

   (3)

6. Who are the leaders in your church or organization with convening power?

   1) Positional?

   2) Practical?

   3)Personal?

7. Reflect on Simone Weil's description of love as attention: "Not only does the love of God have attention for its substance; the love of our neighbor, which we know to be the same love, is made of this same substance."[I] What occupies your attention the most? What captivates you? (If you need help, browse your bookshelf, Netflix queue, or podcast feed.)

8. We make the case in this chapter that rest is as spiritual as work and prayer. Do you agree?

- How do you find (and preserve!) margin for rest?

- What types of rest are renewing and fruitful for your life and ministry?

9. Peter Scazzero warns, "Emotionally unhealthy leaders do not practice Sabbath."[II] They do so at the risk of "ministry" replacing God.

- What are the dangers of neglecting sabbath?

- What does responsible sabbath practice look like in your context?

10. Soulful leaders consecrate their work in prayer. Spend some significant time in prayer for yourself, your work, and the church and ministries that you serve.

I. Simone Weil, "Reflections on the Right Use of School Studies with a View to the Love of God," in *Waiting for God*, trans. Emma Craufurd (New York: Harper and Row, 1951), 114.
II. Peter Scazzero, *The Emotionally Healthy Leader: How Transforming Your Inner Life Will Deeply Transform Your Church, Team, and World* (Grand Rapids, MI: Zondervan, 2015), 32.

# Chapter 7: Soulful Leadership in a World of Calendars and Covenants

## *Group Discussion Guide*

1. According to Will Willimon, "Leadership is necessary only if an organization needs to go somewhere and if an organization is accountable to a mission more important than its own survival."[26] We contend that this description fits every Christian church and ministry.

- What is your church or organization's animating mission? (Think back to the earlier discussion of value.)
- Where does your church/organization need to go? (Revisit your conversation about goals.)
- When has your church experienced disappointment in the midst of change like the returned exiles did in Ezra 3:12? How did the congregation and its leaders respond?
- Has busyness ever displaced kingdom-building among your church/organization? How did you overcome this paralysis? Who were the key leaders that catalyzed renewal?

2. The prophethood of all believers championed by Peter in Acts 2:18 brings with it the responsibility to "test the spirits" commended by John in 1 John 4:1. This need is all the more acute in a day when "being prophetic" is often claimed as license to speak insensitively.

- What does it truly mean to speak prophetically?
- How do we discern true prophecy from mere bluster?
- Is there a cost to speaking as a prophet?

---

26. William H. Willimon, *Leading with the Sermon: Preaching as Leadership* (Minneapolis: Fortress Press, 2020), 31.

3. Coordinating power entails both understanding a situation and communicating it clearly. Clear communication is easy when we're delivering good news, but how can soulful leaders faithfully and clearly communicate hard realities? How do we communicate about scarcity, sickness, and loss?

4. Who are your collaborative partners? *(Compile a list of them on the whiteboard or other display.)*
   - Locally?
   - Nationally?
   - Internationally?

5. Are there other potential partners worthy of consideration?
   - How do you discern opportunities for partnership?

   - What criteria shape the nature of fruitful collaborations?

   - How do these partnerships contribute to your overarching purpose?

6. What role does rest play in the consecration of our ministry?

   - How do we preserve space for our leaders (lay and pastoral) to rest with regularity (both weekly and longer-term)?

   - Do we need to adopt any additional "guardrails" or policies to encourage healthy, Christ-honoring rest?

# 8. Tenacity

*We always thank God for all of you when we mention you constantly in our prayers. This is because we remember your work that comes from faith, your effort that comes from love, and your perseverance that comes from hope in our Lord Jesus Christ in the presence of our God and Father.*

**1 Thessalonians 1:2-3**

You can buy almost anything on eBay. For instance, you can buy a bag of Barilla Flour Manitoba Pizza Bread Cake Dough. The product description for this item promises it to be "a very extensible flour, which allows to obtain a dough resistant to long leavening, more tenacious and less prone to deflating."[1] It turns out pizza dough needs some tenacity. For a baker, the "tenacity" of dough is its capacity to resist deformation. Tenacity is one of the components of consistency.

Congregational and organizational soul cultures are like batches of dough. We work the dough of soul culture to present a consistent witness in our communities and before our God. We mix beliefs, attitudes, values, goals, and practices. Like a good pizza dough, we also need some tenacity so that we don't lose our shape or become inconsistent.

Tod Bolsinger calls for "tenacious perseverance" in his book *Tempered Resilience: How Leaders Are Formed in the Crucible of Change*.[2] He writes, "When the Scriptures speak of resilience, the words they most often use are *endurance* and *perseverance*. The Greek word transliterated *hypomone* is used repeatedly to entreat the saints to persevere in faith and faithfulness amid the trials of this world, heaping the highest praise on those who do."[3]

---

1. Barilla, "Flour Type '0' Manitoba" product description, eBay, https://www.ebay.com/itm/354032903345 (accessed December 21, 2022).

2. Tod Bolsinger, *Tempered Resilience: How Leaders Are Formed in the Crucible of Change* (Downers Grove, IL: InterVarsity Press, 2020), 75.

3. Ibid. (emphasis original)

Tenacity is a mark of discipleship. Jesus was tenacious, and when we walk in his steps, we become tenacious as well. This has been true of God's people throughout time. Proverbs 24:16 observes, "The righteous may fall seven times but still get up, but the wicked will stumble into trouble." It is hard for many of us to read that verse and not hear Chumbawamba thunder in our heads, "I get knocked down, but I get up again, you're never gonna keep me down."[4] The writer of Proverbs seems to say that you just can't keep God's people down. We are wired for tenacity. Wisdom literature like Proverbs keenly observes how life *generally* works. Men and women of the covenant are made to get up again. We are wise when we give some attention to this truth. We need to develop our "get up." Tenacity is one of the great needs of the moment and an opportunity to minister to our communities.

The Covid-19 pandemic forced us to think about resilience, particularly as it relates to children and teens. Children's Hospital Colorado, for instance, declared a state of emergency during the pandemic for the mental health of children. Their Chief Medical Officer David Brumbaugh said, "Our kids have run out of resilience. . . . Their tank is empty."[5]

We have had seminary students in formal mentoring settings confess to burnout. These young adults are in their early twenties. They are hardly even kindled, and they already feel burned out. We need tenacity. We need it as individuals, and it needs to be present in our congregational soul culture.

## The "7 Cs" of Tenacity

How do we work tenacity into our souls and our soul culture? We have benefited from the qualitative research done by Professor Kenneth Ginsburg. Ginsburg is a Professor of Pediatrics in the Division of Adolescent Medicine at the Children's Hospital of Philadelphia and the Perelman School of Medicine at the University of Pennsylvania. He studied resilient kids and declared, "Every once in a while, science proves what our grandmothers told us."[6] Ginsburg's Jewish grandmother told him lots of

---

4. Chumbawamba, "Tubthumping," track 1 on *Tubthumper* (1997).

5. Quoted by Carina Julig, "Children's Hospital Colorado declares 'state of emergency' for pediatric mental health," *Aurora Sentinel*, May 30, 2021, available at *Aspen Times*, https://www.aspentimes.com/news/childrens-hospital-colorado-declares-state-of-emergency-for-pediatric-mental-health/.

6. Kenneth R. Ginsburg, *Building Resilience in Children and Teens: Giving Kids Roots and Wings*, 4th ed. (Itasca, IL: American Academy of Pediatrics, 2020), 311–12.

things rooted in Hebrew scripture. When he observed resilient children, he identified seven consistent characteristics. He calls them "the 7 Cs."[7] When we look at them as Christians, we quickly recognize that the 7 Cs conform closely to biblical principles. They are "competence, confidence, connection, character, contribution, coping, and control."[8]

## Competence

We develop tenacity when we operate with competence. Competence is simply the ability to handle situations effectively. Competence comes through actual life experience. Ginsburg says, "Children can't become competent without first developing a set of skills that allows them to trust their judgments, make responsible choices, and face difficult situations."[9] We see this pattern fleshed out in the lives of many biblical characters. We witness it clearly in David's life.

Psalm 78:70-72 reads, "And God chose David, his servant, taking him from the sheepfolds. God brought him from shepherding nursing ewes to shepherd his people Jacob, to shepherd his inheritance, Israel. David shepherded them with a heart of integrity; he led them with the skill of his hands." Skill is competence, and David's skill was one of the reasons he led with tenacity.

First Samuel 17 records the story of David and Goliath. This widely known narrative illustrates skill development and its contribution to tenacious action. David visited Israel's war camp in the Elah Valley. The great Philistine champion Goliath was blistering the people with insults and taunts. He pleaded for a fight. This distressed Saul and all of Israel with him. Goliath had taunted them for over a month by the time David arrived to visit his brothers. When David witnessed this spectacle, he pushed through his brothers' objections and approached the king. David said, "Don't let anyone lose courage because of this Philistine! . . . I, your servant, will go out and fight him!" (1 Sam 17:32). Saul was ready to brush off the offer. He thought of David as a child. How could Saul send him to fight a warrior? David's response is illustrative:

7. Ibid., 28.

8. Ibid.

9. Ibid., 42.

> Your servant has kept his father's sheep, . . . and if ever a lion or a bear came and carried off one of the flock, I would go after it, strike it, and rescue the animal from its mouth. If it turned on me, I would grab it at its jaw, strike it, and kill it. Your servant has fought both lions and bears. This uncircumcised Philistine will be just like one of them because he has insulted the army of the living God. (1 Sam 17:34-36)

He was bold to face Israel's challenge in part because he had a history of developing competency.

Retired Colonel Don Riley walked into the church office a dozen years ago. He had a copy of the *Wall Street Journal* under his arm. After a short talk, it became clear that Don was going to include a trip to First Baptist Church Waco in his daily list of things to do as a retired man. I said, "Well, Don, if you're going to come anyway, will you leave me your paper?" Colonel Riley has given me a newspaper nearly every day since. I have enjoyed his visits and count him a friend. Don also gave me a book he has given to more than 300 people, Admiral William H. McRaven's *Make Your Bed: Little Things That Can Change Your Life . . . And Maybe the World.* Colonel Riley is a firm believer in the book's simple message. McRaven said, "Nothing can replace the strength and comfort of one's faith, but sometimes the simple act of making your bed can give you the lift you need to start your day and provide you the satisfaction to end it right."[10]

I'm the last one to be legalistic about bed making. Most days it seems like a waste of time, to be perfectly honest. But I have learned the importance of attention to the little things. Author and minister Robert Fulghum famously irons his shirts.[11] I make a perfect peanut butter and jelly sandwich. I love the notion that exercising competence in small things leads to competence in big things. Jesus honored this principle in the parable of the valuable coins recorded in Matthew 25. He said of the servants who skillfully turned a profit on their master's money, "Excellent! You are a good and faithful servant! You've been faithful over a little. I'll put you in charge of much. Come, celebrate with me" (Matt 25:21). If we want to go big, we must learn to think little. When we consistently demonstrate competence, we grow more tenacious. We do this because we feel the pleasure of the Lord.

---

10. William H. McRaven, *Make Your Bed: Little Things That Can Change Your Life . . . And Maybe the World* (New York: Grand Central Publishing, 2017), 9–10.

11. See "Robert Fulghum—Ironing," Inspiration and Spirit, YouTube, https://www.youtube.com/watch?v=rSZugzNnq_0.

## *Confidence*

Christians have a unique understanding of confidence that emerges from our beliefs. Instead of championing a concept of *self*-confidence, Christians embrace *Christ*-confidence. This confidence contributes to tenacity. One of the key texts that teaches Christ-confidence is 2 Corinthians 1:8-11:

> Brothers and sisters, we don't want you to be unaware of the troubles that we went through in Asia. We were weighed down with a load of suffering that was so far beyond our strength that we were afraid we might not survive. It certainly seemed to us as if we had gotten the death penalty. This was so that we should have confidence in God, who raised the dead, instead of ourselves. God rescued us from a terrible death, and he will rescue us. We have set our hope on him that he will rescue us again, since you are helping with your prayer for us. Then many people can thank God on our behalf for the gift that was given to us through the prayers of many people.

An old Southern saying goes, "God won't give you more than you can handle." I jokingly refer to sayings like this one as "Hezekiah 3:16." It sounds biblical and gets quoted like Scripture, but something is just off. Jason Isbell sings a line that folds it in: "Mama says God won't give you too much to bear. Might be true in Arkansas, but I'm a long, long way from there."[12] That might not even be true in Arkansas. According to 2 Corinthians 1:8-11, some things allowed in our lives are indeed too much for us to handle on our own. They aren't, however, too much for the God who raises the dead.

Paul learned to trust God. He also learned that other believers stir the confidence to continue pursuing the purposes of the kingdom. He told the Corinthians that his confidence in God was due in part to their intercessory prayers. We need others because life is hard. Listen to Paul's challenges:

> I've been on many journeys. I faced dangers from rivers, robbers, my people, and Gentiles. I faced dangers in the city, in the desert, on the sea, and from false brothers and sisters. I faced these dangers with hard work and heavy labor, many sleepless nights, hunger and thirst, often without food, and in the cold without enough clothes. Besides all the other things

12. Jason Isbell and the 400 Unit, "Last of My Kind," track 1, *The Nashville Sound*, 2017.

> I could mention, there's my daily stress because I'm concerned about all the churches. (2 Cor 11:24-28)

Paul experienced acute *and* chronic stresses. He was able to continue because of God's presence and God's people. He said so explicitly. After soberly acknowledging challenges, he said, ". . . God comforts people who are discouraged, and he comforted us by Titus's arrival" (2 Cor 7:6).

We comfort each other in our discouragement by reminding each other of the hope of the gospel. God raised Jesus from the dead. God will raise us. Christ came to redeem us. He has promised to come again. We are a people of hope; therefore, we can be a Christ-confident people. We are not immune from life-crushing, discouraging realities. These things assault our confidence and blunt our tenacity. Therefore, we need Christ-confidence.

John Claypool had a long and fruitful pastoral ministry in two denominations. He experienced life-crushing, discouraging events. He suffered loss again and again, but he kept going. He demonstrated tempered tenacity born of Christ-confidence. Claypool often said, "The worst things are never the last things."[13] This clearly sums up Christian hope. The God who is God raises the dead. We can have confidence because we have God and God's promise.

## *Connection*

Tenacious, resilient people share meaningful connections with others. We have some advantages here as Christians. Connecting with others is a fundamental part of our faith. The writer of Hebrews wrote to a group of Christians who were under tremendous pressure to stop following Christ. Their love for Jesus led to financial and physical threats. Hebrews is about the supremacy of Christ. Hebrews shouts, "He's worth it!" Part of what the writer wanted was for the pressured Christians to stay meaningfully connected to one another. The key text is Hebrews 10:19-25:

> Brothers and sisters, we have confidence that we can enter the holy of holies by means of Jesus's blood through a new and living way that he opened up for us through the curtain, which is his body, and we have a great high priest over God's house. Therefore, let's draw near with a

13. John Claypool, "The Worst Things Are Never the Last Things," *30 Good Minutes*, Program 4523, February 2002, available at https://www.youtube.com/watch?v=3g-RrQ6gLpA.

> genuine heart with the certainty that our faith gives us, since our hearts are sprinkled clean from an evil conscience and our bodies are washed with pure water. Let's hold on to the confession of our hope without wavering, because the one who made the promises is reliable. And let us consider each other carefully for the purpose of sparking love and good deeds. Don't stop meeting together with other believers, which some people have gotten into the habit of doing. Instead, encourage each other, especially as you see the day drawing near.

Entering the presence of God is not a feat of strength or cunning. This is often how it goes in adventure films. Hobbits, Goonies, and Indiana Jones himself faced barred entrances and had to overcome by their wit. In contrast to such physical obstacles, our sin barricaded us from the presence of God, and no effort on our part could overcome it. The gospel of God teaches that God's grace overcame our impotence. We have confidence to enter by the blood of Christ. By faith we are sprinkled clean and washed. We have access to God with certainty. One implication of this breathtaking truth is that we are to gather consistently with one another to encourage each other to love and good deeds. We are to spark love by connecting with one another. Sparked love is tenacity.

The writer of Hebrews recognized that not connecting can become habitual. It is a habit we can get into and one we need to avoid. When we don't meet, we don't spark love. This neglect harms others and eventually kills our own tenacity.

The pandemic, growing secularism, and technology have all fertilized the habit of not connecting. Our church is participating in a university-based research project called "Exploring the Pandemic's Impact on Congregations." One of the survey questions asks, "If Covid-19 was not a concern, would you prefer attending worship in person or online?" That's quite a question when you think about it. Many people have concluded that worship is a product that we consume rather than an event in which we participate. Once that mental shift is made, then worship becomes a matter of personal preference. While we do receive in Christian gatherings, we are also called to contribute. That some prefer to consume worship from a distance is a symptom of soul sickness.[14] We are grateful for technology and

---

14. We reiterate here that we are addressing those who *prefer* to opt out of gathered worship. This group is distinct from those whose life circumstances hinder their attendance and full participation, whether for a season or chronically. Every church includes a group of such "providentially hindered" people, and we acknowledge them

use it in ministry. We also recognize that tremendous care must be given to communicate a biblical understanding of Christian connection.

The New Testament is full of letters. These epistles are examples of first-century technology utilized for ministry. The church has always used some form of mediated communication to augment and support face-to-face interactions. But from the beginning, the apostles and the churches that they established viewed face-to-face communication as a superior form of connection. John said so multiple times. One example is 2 John 12: "I have a lot to tell you. I don't want to use paper and ink, but I hope to visit you and talk with you face to face, so that our joy can be complete." We simply can't lose the essential, fundamental Christian practice of consistent connection with other believers.

## *Character*

Christian character is rooted in the gospel because the gospel restores us to our true selves. Paul wrote in Romans 5:1-5,

> Therefore, since we have been made righteous through his faithfulness, we have peace with God through our Lord Jesus Christ. We have access by faith into this grace in which we stand through him, and we boast in the hope of God's glory. But not only that! We even take pride in our problems, because we know that trouble produces endurance, endurance produces character, and character produces hope. This hope doesn't put us to shame, because the love of God has been poured out in our hearts through the Holy Spirit, who has been given to us.

Kenneth Ginsburg said of resilient children, "Resilience is a quality that's part of the original."[15] Character and its resulting tenacity come from being created in the image of God. The gospel restores this original character. Søren Kierkegaard could therefore say, "Now, by the help of God, I shall become myself."[16]

---

with compassion. These folks "would be actively engaged in the church community if they were solely in control of the situation. We [feel] for them, because we [love] them" (Matt Snowden, "Falling Seed: How Mr. Bud's prayers get me through COVID," *Baptist Standard*, April 27, 2021, https://www.baptiststandard.com/falling-seed/how-mr-buds-prayers-get-me-through-covid/).

15. Ginsburg, *Building Resilience*, 41.

16. Søren Kierkegaard, *Søren Kierkegaard's Journals and Papers*, vol. 5, *Autobiographical: Part One, 1829–1848*, ed. and trans. Howard V. Hong and Edna H. Hong

Few people in history developed character and resilience through gospel confidence like Martin Luther. Carl Beckwith contributed a chapter to the book *Biblical and Theological Visions of Resilience* titled "The Certainty of God's Promises: Martin Luther's Pastoral Use of the Gospel."[17] In it he wrote of the transformational power of gospel certainty. Beckwith says, "Believers find resilience amidst the difficulties of life by trusting in the certain promises of God given to them in the word."[18] This confidence forms character and endurance and hope.

We were present the night Alistair Begg delivered his famous "The Man on the Middle Cross" sermon.[19] I had the pleasure of introducing him as we hosted the National Preaching Conference for Baylor's Truett Seminary. A clip from the message went viral on the internet. It has reached viewers the world over and has spawned a cottage industry of Christian merchandise. Type "The man on the middle cross" in a search engine and see what happens.

We believe the message had the impact it did because of the longing for assurance and hope that is in every human heart. Begg winsomely said,

> So to go to the old Fort Lauderdale question, "If you were to die tonight and you were getting entry into heaven, what would you say?" If you answer that, and if I answer it, in the first person, we've immediately gone wrong. "Because I . . . . Because I believed . . . . Because I have faith . . . . Because I am this . . . . Because I am continuing . . . ."
>
> Loved ones, the only proper answer's in the third person. "Because he! Because he!"
>
> Think about the thief on the cross . . . . I can't wait to find that fellow one day to ask him, "How did that shake out for you? Because you were cussing the guy out with your friend. You've never been in a Bible study. You never got baptized. You didn't know a thing about church membership, and yet you made it! You made it! How did you make it?"

---

(Bloomington, IN: Indiana University Press, 1978), 443.

17. Carl L. Beckwith, "The Certainty of God's Promises: Martin Luther's Pastoral Use of the Gospel," in *Biblical and Theological Visions of Resilience: Pastoral and Clinical Insights*, ed. Nathan H. White and Christopher C. H. Cook (London: Routledge, 2020), 139–52.

18. Ibid., 151.

19. Alistair Begg, "The Man on the Middle Cross," sermon, National Preaching Conference, George W. Truett Theological Seminary, Waco, TX, November 20, 2019.

> That's what the angel must have said, you know: "What are you doing here?"
>
> "I don't know."
>
> "What do you mean, you don't know?"
>
> "I don't know."
>
> "Excuse me, let me get my supervisor." They go get their supervisor angel. "So, just a few questions for you. First of all, are you clear on the doctrine of justification by faith?"
>
> The guy says, "I've never heard of it in my life."
>
> "Well let's just go to the doctrine of Scripture immediately."
>
> This guy's just staring, and eventually, in frustration, the supervisor says, "On what basis are you here?"
>
> And he said, "The man on the middle cross said I can come."
>
> That is the only answer.[20]

God's grace is the basis of our character and the animating power of its practical development. Gospel certainty generates godly tenacity, endurance. When we trust God, God becomes our mighty fortress and unfailing bulwark. Right belief is truly transforming. Charles Spurgeon said it well: "If we have believed in Christ aright the Holy Ghost has come upon us to transform us altogether."[21] Through this transformation God makes us our true selves.

## *Contribution*

Tenacity grows when we use our competence and character to contribute to the mission of the community to which God has called us. When God works in a person's life and in church, positive contributions are made. First Peter 4:10-11 says, "And serve each other according to the gift each person has received, as good managers of God's diverse gifts. Whoever speaks should do so as those who speak God's word. Whoever serves does so from the strength that God furnishes . . . ." We should speak and serve for God's glory and the good of others. When we do this, we build confidence and competence. We make a difference and inspire others.

---

20. Ibid., available at https://www.youtube.com/watch?v=xk9wgJBoEd8.

21. Charles Haddon Spurgeon, "Receiving the Holy Ghost," July 13, 1884, in *Metropolitan Tabernacle Pulpit*, vol. 30, available through The Spurgeon Center for Biblical Preaching at Midwestern Seminary, https://www.spurgeon.org/resource-library/sermons/receiving-the-holy-ghost/#flipbook/.

Martin Luther King Jr. contributed. He used his gifts of leadership and preaching to change a nation. King valued tenacity. When he recruited volunteers to the civil rights movement, they had to sign a pledge of nonviolence and ongoing prayer for themselves and the movement with "a will to persevere."[22] When King contributed his gift and gave his life, he inspired others to contribute theirs as well. One such inspired contributor is Thomas Dexter Jakes.

Homiletics professor Frank Thomas once described T. D. Jakes as "undeniably, one of the most nationally and globally imitated preachers in the digital age."[23] His reach is wide, and his influence is deep. It didn't start out that way. Jakes was raised in poverty on the end of a dirt road in Charleston, West Virginia. His hard-working parents provided a simple house, and the one luxury was a small television set. Jakes recalls sitting on a ragged couch watching *Lassie* and the *Andy Griffith Show*. One night the television changed his life as Martin Luther King Jr. appeared on the six o'clock news. Jakes describes the impact like this:

> No matter what his adversaries did to him, he just kept on speaking! His courage was remarkable. His cadence was legendary. It was then that I first realized the power of a man with a microphone. I'm not sure how to quantify the level of this impression on me as a child. Was it his message that moved me? Or maybe it was my father's rapt gaze at him? Whatever the allure, that night left me with one unforgettable takeaway: *A man with a microphone could change the world!*[24]

Making a contribution through speech or service leads others to do the same. It builds tenacity by creating vibrancy in life. Contributing leads to the satisfied tired of excitement and not the lethargy that comes from acedia. Contributing is an antidote to the social toxin known as boredom.

Boredom wearies the soul and is a breeding ground for sin. Walker Percy had a great insight concerning boredom. He said, "The word *boredom* did not enter the language until the eighteenth century. No one knows its etymology. One guess is that *bore* may derive from the French verb *bourrer*,

22. Martin Luther King, Jr., *Why We Can't Wait* (Boston: Beacon Press, 1963), 69.

23. T. D. Jakes, with Frank Thomas, *Don't Drop the Mic: The Power of Your Words Can Change the World* (New York: FaithWords, 2021), 339.

24. Ibid., 15.

to stuff. . . . Boredom is the self being stuffed with itself."[25] We overcome boredom and build tenacity when the Holy Spirit fills us and others are in our hearts. Contributing leads to endurance.

## *Coping*

One of the great opening sentences in the history of book-making belongs to M. Scott Peck. He begins *The Road Less Traveled* with the three-word line, "Life is difficult."[26] Everyone has a wagon to pull. Henry Wadsworth Longfellow said it well: "Believe me, every heart has its secret sorrows, which the world knows not, and oftentimes we call a man cold when he is only sad."[27] Most everyone you meet carries some type of sadness. If we don't learn to cope, we won't be able to persevere.

In chapter 3 we explored Elijah and his sad discouragement. He was at the end of himself. God ministered to him physically, emotionally, mentally, spiritually, and socially. When Elijah couldn't handle life, he learned that God could. Coping is not about heroic efforts. Coping is about being ruthlessly honest regarding our need.

Thomas Merton spoke an honest word to the Lord in his Prayer of Unknowing. Merton prayed,

> My Lord God, I have no idea where I am going. I do not see the road ahead of me. I cannot know for certain where it will end. Nor do I really know myself, and the fact that I think I am following your will does not mean that I am actually doing so. But I believe that the desire to please you does in fact please you. And I hope I have that desire in all that I am doing.[28]

Honest praying helps us cope, and coping helps us persevere.

---

25. Walker Percy, *Lost in the Cosmos: The Last Self-Help Book* (New York: Noonday Press, 1983), 70–71.

26. M. Scott Peck, *The Road Less Traveled: A New Psychology of Love, Traditional Values, and Spiritual Growth*, 25th Anniversary Edition (New York: Simon & Schuster, 2002), 15.

27. Henry Wadsworth Longfellow, *Hyperion: A Romance*, vol. 2 (New York: Samuel Colman, 1839), 39.

28. Thomas Merton, *Thoughts in Solitude* (New York: Farrar, Straus and Giroux, 1999), 79.

If we are completely honest, we don't always have the desire to please God. Perhaps we should own up in prayer and confess that as well. Sometimes this is how transformation begins. David Foster Wallace narrates something like this edgy hope in his rambling novel *Infinite Jest.* One of the main characters is a man named Don Gately. Gately is a character in a residential treatment center for drug addiction. Wallace has him introducing himself to new patients like this:

> He'll tell them right out that he'd first come to Ennet House only to keep out of jail, and hadn't much interest or hope about actually staying clean for any length of time; and he'd been up-front with Pat Montesian about this during his application interview. The grim honesty about his disinterest and hopelessness was one reason Pat even let such a clearly bad-news specimen into the House on nothing but a lukewarm referral from a P.O. up at the 5th District office in Peabody. Pat told Gately that grim honesty and hopelessness were the only things you need to start recovering from Substance-addiction, but that without these qualities you were totally up the creek. Desperation helped also . . . .[29]

Elijah was desperate. He was grimly honest with God. The God of the exodus helped him cope. The God of Easter will help us cope. Coping with life's challenges and reasons for sadness will help us persevere with God-honoring tenacity.

## *Control*

Self-control is a fruit of the Spirit (see Gal 5:22-23). Growing in self-control leads to tenacity. Second Peter 1:5-8 also teaches us about self-control. It says,

> This is why you must make every effort to add moral excellence to your faith; and to moral excellence, knowledge, and to knowledge, self-control; and to self-control endurance; and to endurance, godliness; and to godliness, affection for others; and to affection for others, love. If all these are yours and they are growing in you, they'll keep you from becoming inactive and unfruitful in the knowledge of our Lord Jesus Christ.

---

29. David Foster Wallace, *Infinite Jest* (Boston: Little, Brown and Company, 1996), 464.

Notice how self-control contributes to endurance, which leads to action and fruitfulness.

Self-control is a hard sell because it can sound cold and joyless. I once heard a friend say, "I refuse to exercise, but I love to play." The New Testament has something of this same attitude. Paul especially likes to use images from sports to teach self-discipline. The writer of Hebrews does so as well. When we look at both 1 Corinthians 9:24-27 and Hebrews 12, we see the apostles describe the Christian life as exciting athletic contests. The distance run may be the most helpful image in helping us understand tenacity-inducing self-control.

Professor Angela Duckworth embraces the image of the race. She says, "Grit is living life like it's a marathon, not a sprint."[30] I wonder if she's ever read Hebrews 12:1-2:

> So then, with endurance, let's also run the race that is laid out in front of us, since we have such a great cloud of witnesses surrounding us. Let's throw off any extra baggage, get rid of the sin that trips us up, and fix our eyes on Jesus, faith's pioneer and perfecter. He endured the cross, ignoring the shame, for the sake of the joy that was laid out in front of him, and sat down at the right side of God's throne.

There is joy in the journey *and* joy in the destination. Self-control is ridding ourselves of sin and running the race God has for us. We can do it because Jesus did it, and he's the prototype of a renewed humanity. We can do it because a wonderful cloud of witnesses is cheering us on.

I once read an article in an endurance runners' magazine. It was about the folks who line race roads to cheer on runners, particularly the signs they hold. One guy was shirtless. He had a pair of trousers resting on his ankles. He held a strategically placed sign that said, "Run faster or I'll drop the sign." One elderly woman with a tiny yappy dog held a sign that said, "Keep running or she'll attack." Some held the simple message, "You can do it." Runners confess that they probably couldn't complete their races without the encouragement.

Self-control does not depend on the self. Folks with control look to Christ and consider the witnesses. Playful self-control contributes to tenacity.

---

30. Angela Duckworth, "Grit: The Power of Passion and Perseverance," *TED*, May 9, 2013, https://www.youtube.com/watch?v=H14bBuluwB8.

## Rhino Leadership

Kenneth Ginsburg's qualitative research revealed what God's people have always known: resilience is developed. We are grateful for parents and mentors who instilled this idea in us when we were young and new to ministry. One of these mentors told me (Matt) as a rookie pastor that a pastor needs to be like a rhinoceros. Rhinos have a thick skin and a big heart. This mentor wanted me to be tender and tough, knowing that I would need both for ministry longevity. I was in a Pearl, Mississippi, Kroger's grocery store soon after he gave me the rhino talk. They had a little stuffed rhino in the toy aisle. I brought Rusty the Rhino home, and he took up residence on the corner of my study desk. When congregants asked about him, I told them the story. Over the years my crash of office rhinos has grown. (Did you know a herd of rhinos is called a *crash*?) I've purchased some, but most were gifts from church members, friends all. They are daily reminders that tenacity must animate the work of God.

I recently learned that my old mentor likely borrowed his rhino lesson from Charles Spurgeon. Spurgeon once counseled his own mentees, "To be a successful pastor, one must have the mind of a scholar, the heart of a child, and the hide of a rhinoceros."[31] He wanted them to be thoughtful, tenderhearted, and tough. When we accept the call to lead God's people, we must grow in tenacity. If we are open to it, God will stir this quality in us because God loves tenacity for all the good it does.

31. Quoted by Larry J. Michael, *Spurgeon on Leadership: Key Insights for Christian Leaders from the Prince of Preachers* (Grand Rapids, MI: Kregel, 2010), 169.

Chapter 8

# Tenacity

## Questions for Further Reflection

1. Use a concordance or digital Bible to search for the words "perseverance" and "endurance" in the Scripture. Jot down some notes about what stands out to you from these passages.

2. Have you ever felt that your spiritual and emotional tank was empty? How did you respond? What resources helped you to recover (or could help you to recover if you find yourself in that place now)?

3. Kenneth Ginsburg attributes resilience to "the 7 Cs." Jot some notes about each one of these in your life. Circle the one where you feel strongest. Then underline the one that could use the most growth.

(1) Competence

(2) Confidence

(3) Connection

(4) Character

(5) Contribution

(6) Coping

(7) Control

4. We offer David as a biblical example of competence. What other characters from Scripture demonstrate this quality?

5. Admiral William McRaven recommends making your bed as a simple discipline to frame your day. What simple tasks do you perform regularly to give your day structure and satisfaction?

6. Paul records battling both acute and chronic stresses in 2 Corinthians 11:24-28. Reread that text and then record your own anxieties in each of these categories. After you've written them down, take them to the Lord in prayer. If you're willing, share them with another believer who can intercede for you.

| Acute Stress | Chronic Stress |
| --- | --- |
| | |

7. We contend that every believer contributes something unique to gathered worship (whether they ever step foot on the platform or not). What do you offer when you participate in worship? What do you receive?

8. When we contribute to the work of the kingdom, we can enjoy the "satisfied tired" of service. When have you felt this satisfaction of hard work done for the sake of the gospel?

# Chapter 8: Tenacity

## *Group Discussion Guide*

*Chapter 8 began with a discussion of pizza dough. We recommend enjoying some pizza together as part of this conversation.*

1. How do we comfort one another through seasons of difficulty? How does this comfort instill confidence in one another?

2. Are there members of your church or organization who have neglected connection and "stop[ped] meeting together with other believers, which some people have gotten into the habit of doing" (Heb 10:25)? *(If the social dynamics of your gathering permit, list some of these people by name within small groups.)*

- Are these people "providentially hindered," i.e., prevented from gathering for worship and fellowship by circumstances beyond their control? Or have they simply "gotten into the habit" of remaining away as Hebrews warns against?
- Pray for the people in each of these categories. Then, consider some practical ways to minister and connect with the providentially hindered during the coming week. *(This care may come within existing ministry frameworks or may call for some fresh ideas.)* Next, develop some ideas about how to reach out to those who have disengaged by choice and draw them back into fellowship.

3. The letters of the New Testament are an example of first-century technology used to mediate ministry across physical distance. What technologies does your church or organization use to communicate, collaborate, and commune? How do we keep these technologies in the asset column to facilitate and encourage connection rather than the liability column that distracts or tempts people away from gathering together?

4. Is your church or organization a place where people can be honest about their struggles to cope? Could a church member or guest disclose their

"secret sorrows"[32] or pray Thomas Merton's Prayer of Unknowing? How would others respond?

5. The New Testament regularly compares the Christian life to an athletic contest, especially a race. We resonate with our friend who said, "I refuse to exercise, but I love to play." How does your church or ministry play? What activities stretch and even strain your ministry muscles but also bring delight and adventure? Have you ever experienced a "runner's high" of gospel service and witness?

6. How do we encourage and exhort one another in ministry like the spectators at a marathon race? How can we do so more effectively?

7. Rhinos are tenacious beasts with thick skins and large hearts and therefore serve as mascots for ministry tenacity. (I have a pen-and-ink sketch of one on the desk beside me as I write.) In small groups, discuss the following:

- Does the thick skin or the big heart come more readily for you?
- What's the danger of one without the other?
- How can you grow in each of these tenacious rhino virtues?

32. Henry Wadsworth Longfellow, *Hyperion: A Romance*, vol. 2 (New York: Samuel Colman, 1839), 39.

# 9. Technique, Temperature, and Time: Soul Culture Conversations with Pastors Steve Bezner, Maddie Rarick, and Ralph West

> *Since there is one loaf of bread, we who are many are one body. . . .*
>
> 1 Corinthians 10:17

> *We were all baptized by one Spirit into one body, whether Jew or Greek, or slave or free, and we all were given one Spirit to drink.*
>
> 1 Corinthians 12:13

Baptist pioneer J. B. Gambrell provided the guiding metaphor for our project in his essay "Working a Batch of Dough." In it he counseled, "If we are wise, we will work our dough."[1] Gambrell's fertile image adapted from the pages of Scripture has animated pastoral imagination in his generation and our own. Imagining our congregations as lumps of dough where distinct ingredients combine to form more than the sum of their parts has enabled us to tease out the elements that form a healthy, hopeful soul culture. The ingredients of beliefs, attitudes, values, goals, and practices must all mix with proper purity and proportion for the dough to rise.

But if we consider only our ingredients, we overlook the central point of Gambrell's metaphor: "If we are wise, we will *work* our dough." Baking

---

1. J. B. Gambrell, "Working a Batch of Dough," in *Parable and Precept* (New York: Revell, 1917), 63.

requires more than just the precise combination of flour, water, salt, soda, and yeast. Contestants on competitive baking shows all access the same pantry of pristine ingredients and often work from the same recipe. The best ingredients rightly measured are necessary but insufficient for a first-rate loaf. What distinguishes world-class pastry chefs from more modest bakers is *how* they work their dough. Alongside quality ingredients in the mixing bowl, *technique*, *temperature*, and *time* are absolutely essential.

Working the dough of soul culture is no different. Healthy beliefs, attitudes, values, goals, and practices are essential ingredients for a culture that honors the Lord. Wise leaders knead these ingredients using the proper techniques, heat the mixture to the appropriate temperature, and pace all of these actions for the right time. Think of these as the soft skills of cultural formation, the touch and timing of wise leadership. Since these skills are much more readily caught than taught, we share reflections in this concluding chapter from friends and partners in ministry about how they incorporate the ingredients of soul culture within their respective congregations. All three are Baptist pastors in Texas, but they serve in three distinct ministry settings and represent contrasting stages of pastoral experience and development. We begin with a case study illustrating technique for integrating the ingredients of soul culture.

## Technique

When it comes to kneading dough, technique is paramount. If you've ever attempted an heirloom family recipe (and we hope that all of you have!), you've likely been disappointed when your cornbread didn't come out *quite* like Granddaddy's or your chili was missing a little something that Me-Maw's always had. Take heart! Not even culinary wizards are immune to these frustrations. Alton Brown is one of America's best-known cooking personalities and made a name for himself by highlighting the science behind beloved recipes. Think of him as the Bill Nye of the kitchen. Yet even with his training and attention to detail, the secret of his Ma Mae's biscuits eluded him (although that didn't stop him from featuring the recipe—and Ma Mae herself—in the inaugural season of his Food Network series *Good Eats*).[2] Even rolling out and working their dough side by side with identical ingredients, something was different. Only after Ma Mae's passing did Alton realize the secret to her technique. Her arthritis forced

2. *Good Eats*, season 1, episode 7, "The Dough Also Rises," aired August 18, 1999, on Food Network.

her to work her dough with flat palms instead of using her fingers to knead like Alton did. This nearly invisible change transformed the entire recipe. As Alton reflected two decades after filming his original biscuit episode, "The answer's almost always technique. . . . It's those little things that once they go into the oven grow exponentially into a really big difference."[3]

The answer is almost always technique, and just like cooks, pastors and other ministry leaders refine their techniques over time. Trial and error, experimentation and improvisation lead to improved handling of the five core ingredients of soul culture. Our friend Dr. Steve Bezner offers a tremendous case study of this process in action from the annual planning exercises of Houston Northwest Church where he pastors. Although the planning process naturally foregrounds goals and practices, beliefs, attitudes, and values all play critical parts as well.

Steve came to Houston Northwest a decade ago, and under his leadership the church has grown into a large, multiethnic neighborhood congregation serving one of America's largest and most diverse cities. Their church year runs from August 1 through July 31, intentionally structured to coincide with school calendars.[4] Steve and his team have recognized the disruptions that summertime travel brings to planning processes, so he says, "We have to start it early enough to have it done by Memorial Day, so February is when it begins." The goal of an August 1 kickoff date triggers a cascade of intermediate benchmarks that lead back to a process that began a full six months earlier.

## *Elder Retreat*

Houston Northwest's annual planning begins with a twenty-four-hour retreat by their elders, a group of three ordained staff and four laypeople. Steve credits Jeff Bezos with a practical rule of thumb for team size: "We

---

3. "Good Easts: Reloaded—Ma Mae's Biscuits," promotional video for *Good Eats: Reloaded*, season 1, episode 4, "The Dough Also Rises: The Reload," aired November 5, 2018 on Cooking Channel, available at https://www.facebook.com/CookingChannel/videos/2199575554131941/.

4. We contend that nearly all churches follow this school rhythm, even if their formal church year begins in January with the calendar year, November/December with the Advent launch of the liturgical year, or the October start date of the traditional Baptist calendar. Of course, local factors add further nuance. Matt's brother Mark pastors in an intensely agricultural town in the Texas Panhandle. The cotton crop is so central to life there that soil temperatures during a particular week establish the calendar for the rest of the year.

try to create teams that are no larger than can be fed by two pizzas."[5] They gather at lunch (maybe pizza?) on Friday at a local hotel. With a scant twenty-four hours to accomplish such an ambitious agenda, you might think that the team gets straight to work, and they do—they pray. Beliefs come to the fore from the start of the process. Steve reports that prayer is "basically all we do on Friday. I know that most people when I tell them this think, 'Okay, well you go in and try to steer the conversation.' But I honestly don't."

"So you're really open to what's happening?" we asked him, perhaps a bit incredulous ourselves.

"Exactly, we're just wide open." This radical openness only works in a culture where Christlike attitudes complement biblical beliefs: "People in this room have to be people that you trust, because someone who is manipulative could definitely ramrod this whole process." We returned to this concern later in our conversation and asked Steve how he responds to attempts to control the discernment process with preconceived priorities. He answered that it is a combination of pastoral direction, sanctified peer pressure, and practical leadership:

> I'll typically say something like, "I know that's super important to you, but I want us to be careful that we're not just talking about what's important to us but what the Lord is leading us to do." Most people who are supposed to be in that room receive that direction. If they don't, then you're probably not going to invite them back next year. The other thing is you hopefully have strong leaders in that room. If there are seven of us, there's always one person who's fired up about something, but nobody else is feeling it. If that one person is Spirit-led, they'll recognize, "Okay, I guess that's not the thing this year." Sometimes I've been the one coming in fired up, and if nobody else is, I lay my pet project down. Then that just changes the demeanor in the room. It's not really rocket science. It's really just listening to the Lord and taking the time to bring as many people into the process as you can.

Beliefs and attitudes mingle together in service of values, goals, and eventually practices.

---

5. Quoted in Justin Bariso, "Jeff Bezos Knows How to Run a Meeting. Here's How He Does It," *Inc.*, April 30, 2018, https://www.inc.com/justin-bariso/jeff-bezos-knows-how-to-run-a-meeting-here-are-his-three-simple-rules.html.

After about an hour of prayer, Steve invites elders to share things God placed on their hearts, what their church calls "Holy Spirit impressions." They compile lists on whiteboards or flip charts in the holy space of a hotel conference room and then return to prayer. The exact wording of the prompts varies, but the core process basically repeats itself throughout the afternoon. Before breaking for dinner, the team considers their lists and looks for patterns. Without fail, common themes emerge. Examples from recent years include Bible literacy, evangelism and baptism, marriage and discipleship, the bread-and-butter realities of life together as the church. Steve circles consensus items and then transcribes them onto a final list.

The elders share a nice dinner (not pizza this time!) that evening along with their spouses. The church provides the meal as an expression of gratitude for their investment of time. This token meal is a small thing that's a big thing, a tangible manifestation of the congregation's values.

Saturday morning begins with a brainstorming session about how to pursue the priorities identified the day before in the upcoming year. Some suggestions are great and others are . . . different. The goal at this point is to capture all the ideas and cull for the best later. Steve leads this pivot with the question, "If we could only focus on a couple of these things, what do we think are the best ones?" They refine their goals to three or four and identify one of these as their "Wildly Important Goal," or W.I.G, "the one thing that we are going to ask everyone to work on." This year Houston Northwest decided to focus on baptism. Using a formula developed by Thom Rainer, they set the concrete goal to baptize one hundred people in twelve months. By midday the elder team is ready to depart with three to four goals for the upcoming year including one W.I.G. to rally the church behind.

### *Staff Retreat and Strategy on a Page*

A staff retreat follows about two weeks after the elder retreat. This meeting launches the implementation phase where the Broad Ambitions discerned by the elders take shape as Concrete Plans. Steve unveils the goals adopted by the elders to the rest of the staff and then divides the members into ministry teams to brainstorm implementation ideas. After a five-minute timer sounds, the group reconvenes and writes ideas on the wall. Attitudes of camaraderie and good-natured ribbing come to the fore again as "people are laughing and cutting up as they say, 'That's a good idea; that's a terrible idea.'" Only trusted friends can laugh together as they dismiss one another's terrible ideas. Next, the staff repeats the same process for the same goal in a different group, cross-pollinating among the ministry teams. This lateral brainstorming fosters creativity and ownership of *all* the goals by *all* the ministry staff.

After brainstorming about all the identified goals, Steve instructs each ministry team to think through how they can advance each one in the upcoming year. He explains the importance of this step: "This is helpful because my music guys, for instance, tend to think, 'I just have to pick a song and lead the choir.' Once we ask, 'What would it look like for you in the worship area to make sure that baptisms are highlighted more?' they respond, 'We never thought about that.' We set them loose for an hour to come up with a plan and present it."

Once again, healthy attitudes of collaboration enable staff to give honest feedback: "That's a great idea! . . . That will never work! . . . Have you thought about this? . . . This is pretty good, but you need to tweak that." Steve advises, "Try to make it fun, to laugh."

At the end of the day, every ministry team can say, "Here's a way that we can contribute." Each team remains responsible for the basic tasks in their core ministry portfolio, but they are also invited "to take their eyes off their specific ministry areas and do some things together." Ministry teams leave the staff retreat charged to create a Strategy on a Page (S.O.A.P.). This document is a single-page summary of how their team will advance the church's annual goals between August 1 and July 31. The space limit demands that teams focus, simplify, and communicate clearly. They submit these documents to Pastor Steve by Memorial Day, who reviews and revises each one and then compiles them into his annual Vision Talk.

## *Vision Dinner, Vision Talk*

Vision Talks have become a tentpole tradition at Houston Northwest under Steve's leadership. He delivers this annual "State of the Church" address at a series of dinners at the beginning of August. The carefully crafted structure of these talks looks like this:

I. Last year's vision (about 10 minutes)
  a. Goals A, B, C, D . . .
  b. How we did on each goal and why
II. Current "State of the Church" (about 10 minutes)
  a. Sunday attendance

   b. Financial update
III. Where are we going next year? (the rest of the talk)[6]
   a. Show the brokenness/need
   b. Create a desire to act on it immediately
   c. Present a possible solution
   d. Invite them to join

Steve explains, "If the people see a need and a vision that meets that need, then they want to jump in." In other words, "Show me what doesn't occur if we don't do this. Tell me what makes a difference."

Vision Dinners have become a highly anticipated part of Houston Northwest's calendar by deliberate design. The church pays for the meal and promises a gift for everyone who attends, foregrounding participation in the dinner as a congregational value. Some of the gifts become not only incentives but ongoing advertisements for the event. This year's gift was a shirt with the slogan "In Houston as it is in Heaven." As people noticed their friends wearing the shirts, they asked, "Where did you get that shirt?" These gifts became viral marketing for upcoming years. Meanwhile, the staff complement this implicit invitation with aggressive promotion, including from the pulpit. Along with this broad publicity, the church staff extends personal invitations to key congregational leaders: teachers, ministry directors, deacons, committee leaders, etc. "We know these are the people who are going to be asked questions," explains Steve. "So we do everything we can to get them there," including hosting multiple dinners to fit a variety of schedules and keep the attendance at each one more intimate.

At the end of the meal and Vision Talk, each attendee completes a response card customized to that year's event with their name, contact information, and options "to support the vision of HNW in the upcoming year by . . . ." Options correspond to the particular goals and ministries for that year, such as volunteering to serve in a particular ministry area, joining a group, committing to give generously, etc. Ministry assistants compile these responses and distribute them to the church staff for personal contacts regarding next steps. These connections are especially helpful for the incorporation of the newest church members.

6. Bezner relies heavily on Andy Stanley for the structure of this final section. See Andy Stanley, *Visioneering: Your Guide for Discovering and Maintaining Personal Vision* (Colorado Springs, CO: Multnomah, 2005); Andy Stanley, *Making Vision Stick* (Grand Rapids, MI: Zondervan, 2007).

Houston Northwest's process originates with elders, but one of its appeals is its adaptability to any polity. As we observed in our conversation, every church has its "elders" recognized and affirmed for their wisdom, even if a congregation's polity designates them as deacons or committee chairs rather than the elder title. In churches with a smaller staff than Houston Northwest's, incorporation of more of these deacons or committee leaders at the staff retreat implementation stage may prove helpful. "If I had any counsel," Steve shares, "it would be to make sure that in that first group, include lay leaders." Participation by laypeople at the earliest origins of the discernment process creates organic investment and bears witness to beliefs about the priesthood of all believers.

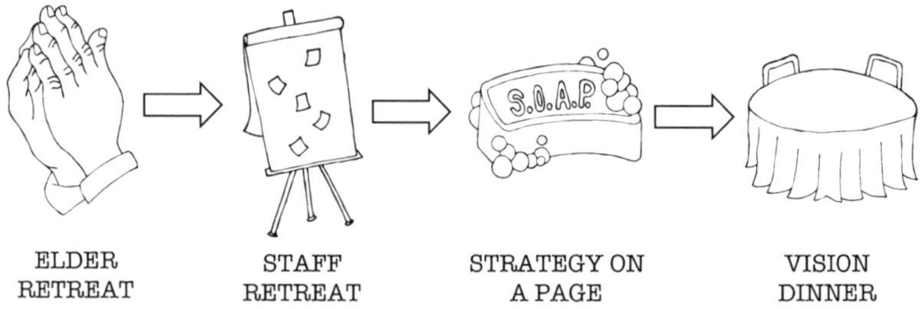


**Figure 5. Houston Northwest Church's Vision Process**

## Temperature

Maddie Rarick is a young pastor six months into her first call. Our church ordained her to gospel ministry upon her call to pastor the Meadow Oaks Baptist Church in Temple, Texas. We drove down Interstate 35 to visit with her, see her church, and catch up about her initial experiences leading a congregation. We noticed signs posted all throughout the church building, but two particularly stood out as bookends of our visit. One of the first impressions we had of Meadow Oaks was a sign pledging that their church "is a Christ-centered community of grace and faith, doing justice, loving kindness, and walking humbly with our God." The congregation has adopted the language of Micah 6:8 as their mission statement, reflecting the translation of beliefs into values and ultimately practices.

As we settled into Maddie's office, our conversation quickly turned to attitudes. "You hear all kinds of war stories when you're in seminary about all the difficulties of ministry," Maddie said. "I have a little bit of a tendency to project the worst possible scenario, so I was assuming that things would be a lot harder or more frustrating than they have been." She's been pleasantly surprised by the warm reception from a congregation eager to welcome her as pastor. Maddie likens the warnings that she received in seminary to the cautions from a parent: "If I were thinking about the next generation, I would want to prepare them for the hardest things and let them be surprised by what's good." Her own testimony, though, indicates that maybe these well-intentioned concerns can be overdone and create unnecessary anxiety or guardedness among first-time pastors. Thankfully, Maddie has embraced her call and her congregation and adopted an attitude of joyfulness, even with a predisposition toward worst-case planning. She reports that her congregation "has just been really supportive, and honestly a lot of fun."

Academic professionals, including theologians and Bible scholars, comprise a disproportionate amount of the Meadow Oaks congregation. These folks readily navigate the conceptual world of belief. The temptation that corresponds to this gift is to remain in abstraction. As she acclimates to the rhythms of weekly preaching, Maddie is learning to translate beliefs into practices. "The beliefs come easily and naturally, like the heart language of the congregation immersed in theology. Practices, action, and engagement really need some attention." Her response has been to push, but to push slowly: "Part of my job if things are going well is to push and to say we can do more than what we're doing. But we're probably going to need to ease into it. Right now we have to take slow steps." These slow steps in gospel directions advance the culture and the kingdom.

As the church ventures into unfamiliar territory, they rely on the values that have held them together throughout their congregation's life. Chief among them is a premium value on congregational life together. Meadow Oaks is adept at "one anothering." Maddie quickly noticed, "This is a group that's weathered a lot of life together. A lot of life. They really know how to take care of each other." This community bondedness reveals itself in times of joy: "We eat together constantly." We noticed in our visit how expansive the fellowship hall was relative to the rest of the facility. Even the church architecture demonstrates how much these people enjoy sharing tables. But the community bonds also reveal themselves in times of crisis: "If somebody is sick or in the hospital, everybody else knows and prays about it. It's a very communicative congregation." The value of fellowship meets belief about prayer and translates into practices of intercession and tangible expressions of care.

The church's high value of one another also manifests in congregational administration and governance practices. "The committees really make the decisions," Maddie reported.

We probed a bit more in light of our recent conversation with Steve Bezner about Houston Northwest's vision process: "What I hear you saying is that you're not pre-arriving at a decision and then working it through the committees. What is your role as pastor in the process?"

"The way that I see myself in committee decisions *is* pastoring," she said. "If we're going over the budget to guide our congregation to be faithful with its resources, that's a theological document." She serves as shepherd in these deliberations, linking preaching, pastoral care, and practical leadership.

Maddie's participation in committee governance offers a case study in leadership. She approached key lay leaders and told them, "I'm happy to come to these meetings. I kind of considered it part of my job. Is that okay?" Their response was unanimously positive. Her gentle request was both simple and savvy. She asked permission but also told her preference. She submitted herself to the will of the larger church while giving a clear indication of her own values and goals in a way that reoriented the church's practices. The church welcomed this directive leadership that continued to respect and maintain its core congregational polity. Meanwhile, other decisions required even more direct action, like when the heat went out on a Sunday morning. The chair of the facilities committee was recovering from knee surgery, so Maddie took the initiative to call the repair company. "I just kind of got it done," she said with a laugh. It turns out that the same churches that value collective decision-making also value heat in the winter. Some choices call for careful consensus building, but some just need a phone call to the HVAC technician. Wise leaders can quickly discern the difference.

As Maddie continues through her first year as pastor, she's beginning to turn her attention toward ministry goals for Meadow Oaks. She described the tension between identifying goals and remaining open to unexpected opportunities that the Lord provides. One priority for the congregation is reaching children and young families, particularly post-pandemic. Maddie shares this goal but also reminds her church from the pulpit, "If we're working to be faithful witnesses, you don't know who will walk through these doors." Goals to reach young people shouldn't eclipse or devalue elders or singles, particularly with the church situated in an aging neighborhood.

Maddie identified goal-setting as "the greatest challenge" in a church of intellectuals. "We can work through the concepts really easily in this congregation," she said, "and think through them deliberately. But we struggle when it comes to making real, tangible goals. It can sometimes feel like the most amorphous thing." For a church at home in the realm of beliefs, the temptation is to remain in perpetual abstraction. Once again, Maddie has learned to push, but push gently. "You can't come in and say, 'Here's the process for goal setting,' in a way that disrupts the system in an unhealthy way." The vision process that Bezner employs at Houston Northwest, for instance, took years to craft and implement.

Meadow Oaks also values stability. Since its founding in the 1950s, the church has never ended a budget year in the red. While this remarkable track record could catalyze bold ventures, it can also hamper them. Plans and goals aren't synonymous; sometimes commitment to a plan can inhibit goals "because you have to go off-script, off the map." This dynamic highlights the creative tension between management and leadership. "I see my job," Maddie said, "as encouraging risks because the management here is so strong." With a proven track record of stability, this young pastor can "perform a highwire act with a really, really sturdy net." Management and leadership complement and free one another. Undergirding both is the anchor of belief: "You can rest in the hope of good theology, that the 'stuff' is true."

The security of sound theology and faithful management enables leaders, lay and pastor alike, to translate goals into practices. "If somebody has an idea for ministry that fits us," Maddie says, "I encourage them to try." This effort is shared by the whole congregation, consistent with Ephesians 4:11-12. "I'm not going to do everything," Maddie said. "That's not laziness; that's empowering a congregation."

The church's ministry to college students provides a perfect example of her use of convening power to mobilize ministry practice. Maddie arrived to find a healthy, growing college ministry in need of a dedicated meeting space. The most natural room was where the youth currently met, "which on paper made ton of sense . . . but we don't live on paper!" Maddie floated the proposal to the chair of the Children and Youth Committee, who also happens to have a teenage child. She quickly discerned sensitivity and told the chairperson, "I need you to think about it. Get back to me in a week." After time to think through the idea, the chairperson agreed, on conditions that the youth continue to have their own space. With this assent and identification of a suitable youth room, Maddie convened leaders of both ministry areas and told them, "Do with it what you will." She exercised convening power as the only person within the system with the authority to call the meeting and begin a conversation. Once she did so, and defused the resulting tensions, "then people were animated to let their gifts flow. . . . Once we came to consensus, the creativity of how it would happen was up to them. I didn't care what color the paint was!"

"So what color did they choose?" we asked.

"This color," Maddie replied, gesturing toward her office walls.

"They chose the color of your office?" we replied, overwhelmed by the subtle affirmation of Maddie's pastoral leadership.

"Well, I chose the office color because it was leftover paint from them," Maddie said, smiling. The real iconography of this leadership practice appeared when we walked upstairs and toured the redesigned college room. Adorning one wall is a mural of the church's logo that depicts praying hands opening into a fruitful tree. Because multiple generations of lay leaders were shepherded through a delicate process to provide college students their own space, these students have recognized themselves as members of a larger whole. The dedicated college room bears visible witness that it belongs to Meadow Oaks, and to Christ.

We walked together toward the exit, passing more mission statement placards in the hallways along with countless other signs that decorate every mid-sized church. As we reached the doorway, we noticed a final sign taped above the handle reminding church members to lock up as the last out of the building. We paused to mention all of these memos of shared ministry responsibility, and Maddie told us about her favorite one: "The oven in the fellowship hall has a card above it that says, 'Heats slowly.'" While slow heating may be a limitation for an electric oven, it seems like a wise word for ministry leadership, especially during year one. As leaders we apply heat. We introduce creative tension into human systems to reinforce belief, refine attitudes, clarify values, articulate goals, and drive practices. But we heat slowly. We handle precious ingredients, and no baker places raw dough beneath a broiler. Scorched crusts and raw centers don't serve the kingdom. Instead, we allow temperature and time to cooperate to transform our congregational ingredients into a savory witness to the world.

## Time

Longevity in ministry is precious, so we conclude with wisdom from a pastor at the opposite end of a pastoral career from Maddie. Dr. Ralph

Douglas West is the founding pastor of The Church Without Walls in Houston, Texas. During his thirty-five-year leadership, this church has grown from a church plant meeting in Ralph's mother's garage into one of the nation's largest and most vibrant congregations. Dr. West is a pastor to pastors, and we are grateful to count him a friend and encourager.

Church Without Walls was born out of a contrast in values. Over four years at his former congregation, "four years of a battle," Ralph recalled, "I was going in one direction and trying to pull them that way, and they were saying, 'We're comfortable in the direction that we're in.'" The disagreement centered on ministry to children and youth. Both pastor and congregation valued young people and ministry to them, but they disagreed over goals and practices to accomplish it. "This church had a long history with youth and children," Ralph said, "but children and youth had changed." He wanted to provide age-specific services "where we could do church on children's level, where they could understand, and youth the same thing, but that was viewed as me not wanting the children and the youth in the church service." The conflict eventually reached a point where Ralph chose to step aside, and Church Without Walls was born, originally known as Brook Hollow Baptist Church.

The church grew exponentially, quickly moving from a garage to a hotel ballroom to a repurposed building to a multi-campus congregation. Ralph attributes this numerical growth, and the more important underlying spiritual growth, to a strong emphasis on evangelism and discipleship. For years Church Without Walls led Texas Baptist churches in completion of the thirteen-week discipleship books provided by the convention. This premium value on discipleship grew from a deep sense of call in the pastor's heart. Ralph grew up in a church that highly emphasized evangelism, and vibrant worship is a hallmark of his Black church tradition. In his words, "We got worship together." These strengths then beg the questions, "How do you disciple people? How do we then promote education?" These questions crystallized for Ralph as a college student during a tour of First Baptist Church of Dallas sponsored by the Bishop College Religion Department. After seeing the sanctuary, educational space, and chapel, a professor called Ralph by name and declared, "Ralph, if you build a building that seats 1,500, you ought to have 1,500 seats for education." Her charge struck home, and Ralph determined, "If I ever build a building, I'm going to have the same amount of seats for education that I have for worship." He elaborated on the need for discipleship: "We have broad churches. We have wide churches. We need *deep* churches." Despite being known as pastor of a large church, Ralph's heart goal is for a deep church.

The practical pillars of Sunday school and deacon family ministry incarnate this discipleship value. Church Without Walls prioritizes connecting people with Sunday school, encouraged by statistics that these small group connections translate into longevity of engaged membership. Ralph smiled as he recalled how many congregants who joined Sunday school groups in their twenties and thirties have remained at Church Without Walls throughout most of his thirty-five years there. These members receive pastoral care from deacons organized by zip codes. These laypeople "became extensions of pastoral ministry" rather than a decision-making body, "the way they should have been in the first place." Throughout the pandemic the deacon body "became the glue to hold things together" by calling the members under their charge time and time again. These deacons enabled the church to "maintain unity and keep some vibrance," even while socially distant and hindered from corporate worship. "Though the pandemic affected literally thousands of people in church attendance," he acknowledged, "we've been able to maintain everything that we needed to do because of the deep roots in the life of those people who took the commands of Christ seriously to go into the world and make disciples." Once again, beliefs rooted in Scripture define values, goals, and practices. "That's been the sustaining principle, because if not, we would be in trouble today. I mean, we really would be in trouble."

Attitudes also play a role, particularly those of the pastor, staff, and deacon leaders. Ralph gave us a modern-day parable: "The leader has two buckets, water and gasoline. If you have some embers and put water on it, you can douse the flame before it even starts. You get somebody with gasoline, they can blow up the place." Every church—just like every other human institution—deals with some smoldering embers from time to time. Prudent leaders can come with a cup of cool water to douse the flame before anyone gets burned. At Church Without Walls, the deacons are the frontlines of this bucket brigade. We liked the image so much that at our own church's annual deacon banquet the next week, we presented our outgoing deacon chair with a bucket of bottled spring water and a gas station gift card in symbolic recognition and thanks for her year of service.

Attitude begins at the top of any organization. Leaders set the emotional temperature for the entire body. As Ralph puts it, "A happy pastor can make a happy church." Happiness might sound trite, but it's not just glee and sunshine for its own sake. Our attitudes become a core ingredient of our gospel witness. "Happy folk want to come to where happy is," Ralph reminded us. "That's why they go to happy hour, trying to manufacture happy! When we have an intoxication from the Spirit, the fruit of the Spirit will spill out of us. People want to be around that. They can't get it anywhere else. They can't get it at work. They can't get it at school. They can't get it."

The Apostle Paul describes that fruit of the Spirit in Galatians 5:22-23, where the second characteristic is joy. Joy is both attractive and contagious. Ralph finds joy in the fellowship of his congregation and looks for it in other ministers: "I just never wanted to be that person that didn't enjoy walking into a room with God's people and experiencing the joy of the Lord. I really believe that joy becomes the one characteristic by which people are able to identify the depth of our relationship with Jesus Christ. I just enjoy to see a pastor stand up and really enjoy it." A joyful ministry also enables faithful delivery of hard words in their season. "It gives permission to the pastor when the pastor has to make a correction," Ralph observed. The congregation can receive that difficult word as one from a loving parent "in the atmosphere of family love and trust."

We asked Ralph to conclude with some words of exhortation to young pastors, with Maddie as our representative model. What counsel does Ralph wish he had heard six months into his own ministry? He arranged his reply around the five soul culture ingredients of beliefs, attitudes, values, goals, and practices. First, he said, "You have to believe deeply that the great stories of the biblical text are here not just to inform people but to form them spiritually. I would say to a young preacher, 'Thank you for all of the information, but let that information transfer into spiritual formation that will prayerfully lead to life transformation.'"

Ralph returned to the fruit of the Spirit to address attitudes, highlighting love and patience. "Preach to them," he said, "but love them. Teach them, but love them. One of the most important practices you will ever exercise as a young pastor is to remember to be patient. Give them time to grow, but be very, very patient. And then when you need to do another thing, be patient. And when you need to do something else, be patient. Be patient." We suspect that Ralph would applaud Maddie's determination to push, but push slowly. As a forty-year veteran, Ralph recognizes the connection between patience and authority. As a beginning pastor, he "thought that authority of the pastor was that you made all the decisions. Nothing moved until you said it." Looking back, he now recognizes that "the reverence of the people allowed" his childhood pastor and role model to lead in such a way. After decades "of preaching, teaching, baptizing, burying, and blessing, the people *have given me the permission to be their pastor.*" Congregations grant this permission "only once you've given yourself over" to the gospel and to them.

Values become the filtering grid to evaluate open doors of opportunity that arise from time to time. The mission of The Church Without Walls is "to bring men and women who do not have a personal relationship with Jesus Christ into fellowship with Him and into responsible church membership through equipping believers, enriching persons, evangelizing people, and edifying missions." Ralph chuckled as he conceded that even with such a clearly articulated mission, "everybody's always got a mission that the Lord has given to them." Whenever a staff member or other leader presents such a "mission," Ralph's first reply is always, "Have you run it through the grid?" In other words, "Does it line up with the vision and mission of the church? Will it bring people without personal relationship into relationship with Christ? Will it make them responsible church members?"

Ralph illustrated this grid with a memorable story from his own family. His nephew is an up-and-coming Houston hip hop artist. Several years ago he called his father, Ralph's brother James, to ask, "Do you think Pastor would have Kanye at the church?"

James replied, "No. . . . But I'll call him."

Ralph nearly always agrees to requests from his brother, "but on this one, I said I wouldn't invite him. What value is he going to add? Does he line up with the values and the beliefs of our church? I see no sign of that, so I cannot invite him. I couldn't even let him lease the building, because it would give the image of support." For Ralph, the proposal was a non-starter, even with the potential upside of a packed house of people disconnected from the church and from Christ. This particular open door didn't even rise to the level of deliberation. No pro/con list needed! "I didn't have to say, 'Let me think about it,'" he reflected. "This doesn't fit. It doesn't go through the grid, so it is a clear 'No.'" Some decisions are hard because the relative opportunities and costs are tough to weigh; others are hard simply because they will be unpopular. Running choices through the grid of values filters out much of the former so that leaders can focus on the latter. While Ralph's decision was unpopular at the time, the intervening years have vindicated the wisdom of preserving the integrity of his ministry.

Once values are clear and secure, leaders can turn their attention toward goals. Ralph emphasized, "Goal setting can be spiritual. It can be a mature activity and an act of faith." He implicitly addressed the concern that setting concrete goals, especially numeric ones, is somehow crass or carnal. He conceives such goals as an invitation "to activate faith, to believe that God is calling me to reach this many people, baptize this many people, disciple this many people." He balances this perspective by keeping goals in their proper place as an aspiration rather than an idol: "What happens if you fall short? It's okay. At least I had a goal." At this stage of ministry, Ralph operates more by intuition than through formalized process. This tendency is likely part experience, part personality. "I don't think strategically," he conceded. He shores up this liability through the help of others. He continued, "I have to have people around me who are strategic. They take what I say, and then they put texture to it and turn it into a strategy. I just don't naturally think that way. I'm on the artistic side of life." The distinction between leadership and management comes up again here. Ralph improvises like a jazz musician but then relies on trusted gospel partners to generate a Strategy on a Page.

All of these ingredients combine to shape practices, but Ralph returned here to the personal world of the pastor's own discipleship. He offered counsel to Maddie, to us, and to all of you readers not to neglect our core spiritual practices before the Lord. "Develop personal practices of your spiritual development and growth," he encouraged. "Try not to let anything interfere with that. Your time of prayer, your time of spiritual reflection and meditation. As a pastor, love your people."

Love is the final word. Churches are complex recipes of beliefs, attitudes, values, goals, and practices. An impurity or omission of any ingredient can sour the entire loaf. Once the ingredients are mixed and kneaded, wise pastors employ technique, temperature, and time to shape and bake the bread. Plan purposefully. Heat slowly. And love your people. As any good baker will allow, the secret ingredient isn't so secret after all. The best recipes are always made with love. As our Lord taught us, "Love each other. Just as I have loved you, so you also must love each other. This is how everyone will know that you are my disciples, when you love each other" (John 13:34-35).

Chapter 9

# Technique, Temperature, and Time

## Soul Culture Conversations with Pastors Steve Bezner, Maddie Rarick, and Ralph West

**Questions for Further Reflection**

1. Steve Bezner describes the annual planning process of Houston Northwest Church, but their process is readily adaptable for individuals or households. Do you set annual goals and priorities for yourself? How might you do so with greater intentionality and especially receptivity to the Holy Spirit? What would a personal planning retreat look like for you?

2. Do you have a Wildly Important Goal? How did you discern it? How are you doing in pursuit of it?

3. What attracted you to your current church? Why did you choose to visit, participate, join, and ultimately serve there?

4. Eugene Peterson, ironically borrowing language from Nietzsche, called the life of discipleship "a long obedience in the same direction."[1] We make similar reference to "slow steps in gospel directions." How do you respond to this sustained, steady pace of kingdom service? Are you encouraged or frustrated by the rate of change within your own life and the life of the community you serve? Are you prepared to "heat slowly"?

1. Eugene Peterson, *A Long Obedience in the Same Direction: Discipleship in an Instant Society* (Downers Grove, IL: InterVarsity Press, 2021).

5. How can you balance identification and pursuit of intentional goals with receptivity to unexpected opportunities that the Lord provides? Reflect on the creative tension between these two sorts of ministry, both personally and in the life of your church or organization.

6. How would you articulate the distinction between management and leadership? Which one is your more natural skill set?

7. Ralph West's visit to First Baptist Dallas while a student at Bishop College crystallized a heart goal within him to pastor a "deep church." Do you have a similar heart goal? Was there a particular moment of clarity when the Lord revealed this call to you?

8. Every leader, according to Pastor West, has two buckets: water and gasoline. We suspect that you've used both at some point. When did you use water to douse a potential fire? When did you pour gasoline onto a volatile situation?

9. Pastor West surrounds himself with gifted strategic thinkers because he recognizes that he operates more "on the artistic side of life." What people has God placed around you to complement your skills and shore up your weaknesses? Thank God for them.

10. Pastor West's primary counsel for young pastors—and by extension, all ministry leaders—is to love people and show patience to them. Spend time in prayer asking the Lord to grow this fruit of the Spirit within you.

# Chapter 9: Technique, Temperature, and Time: Soul Culture Conversations with Pastors Steve Bezner, Maddie Rarick, and Ralph West

## *Group Discussion Guide*

1. Does your family have any heirloom recipes? What have you learned from preparing a dish with a loved one from another generation? Have you ever caught any techniques that don't show up on a recipe card? *(Leaders, consider inviting participants to bring some recipes to share.)*

2. Does your church or organization have a formalized annual planning process?

- If so, diagram it together on butcher paper or a whiteboard and discuss the rationale for each step.
- If not, would you benefit from one? Brainstorm and make a flow chart of some potential steps to consider, guided by the example of Houston Northwest Church.

3. Steve Bezner commends approaching the planning process as a pastoral leader with a blank slate, an openness to what the Spirit reveals through prayer in community. Maddie Rarick, meanwhile, reflects on the responsibility of pastors to shepherd committees and other e church through deliberative processes. How do these two approaches complement and inform one another? How do you discern when open receptivity is needed and when more directive guidance is appropriate?

4. Experiment with the beginning stage of Houston Northwest's planning process. In small groups, perhaps around a table, spend some significant time asking for the Lord's direction and then share any "Holy Spirit impressions" that emerge with one another. Afterward, move forward with these impressions as appropriate within your context and polity.

5. How does your church or organization express gratitude for the contributions of leadership, especially lay leaders (e.g., Houston Northwest's provision of lodging and nice meals during the planning retreat)? Are there additional opportunities to say—and demonstrate—thank you to those who support and guide your shared work?

6. Within your church/organizational structure, how do different personnel/teams collaborate with one another? How can you challenge leaders with contrasting primary responsibilities to share in the pursuit of core objectives? How can you foster cross-pollination across ministry areas?

7. How effectively does your church communicate vision, especially when introducing new ministry priorities? Do you effectively demonstrate need, create a desire to act, present a potential solution, and invite people to participate? Are there any breakdowns or oversights in these steps? In small groups, assign a letter grade to your current vision communication and then make some recommendations about how to improve.

8. As a whole group, brainstorm a list of the signs that people encounter within your church building. What do these signs communicate about your beliefs, attitudes, values, goals, and practices? *(You might divide into teams and conduct a scavenger hunt to see who can identify the most signs throughout the facility or the most unusual example.)*

9. The scale of its fellowship hall communicates one of the key values of Meadow Oaks Baptist Church, a premium on sharing meals together around a common table. What are some of your church's architectural features that reveal collective values? Compile a list together.

10. Is your church or organization more adept at management or leadership? Within a healthy system, these gifts complement and free one another. Is that the case in your setting?

11. The Meadow Oaks college room is a tangible marker of leadership success. What spaces in your setting are analogous examples of growth and life?

12. Ralph West credits the Black church's vibrant worship tradition, saying, "We got worship together." What aspect of ministry does your church "have together"? What do you do especially well within your tradition? Thank God for this gift.

13. "Happy folk want to come where happy is," says Pastor West. Is your church or organization a happy place? What attracted you to it originally?

14. Does your church have a "grid" for evaluating unexpected opportunities or requests? How do you process these spontaneous open doors? Who makes the decision? What criteria do they employ?

15. Conclude with prayer together. Intercede for one another's specific requests. Pray and ask God for wisdom (see Jas 1:5) to work the dough of beliefs, attitudes, values, goals, and practices. Seek the Holy Spirit's technique, temperature, and time to produce a congregational soul culture savory to the Lord and satisfying to a hungry world.